LOOKING FOR LORAX

L. R. DUGAL

Outskirts Press, Inc.
Denver, Colorado

The opinions expressed in this manuscript are solely the opinions of the author and do not represent the opinions or thoughts of the publisher. The author represents and warrants that s/he either owns or has the legal right to publish all material in this book.

Looking for Lorax
All Rights Reserved.
Copyright © 2008 L. R. Dugal
V2.0

Cover Photo © 2008 JupiterImages Corporation. All rights reserved - used with permission.

This book may not be reproduced, transmitted, or stored in whole or in part by any means, including graphic, electronic, or mechanical without the express written consent of the publisher except in the case of brief quotations embodied in critical articles and reviews.

Outskirts Press, Inc.
http://www.outskirtspress.com

ISBN: 978-1-4327-1713-1

Outskirts Press and the "OP" logo are trademarks belonging to Outskirts Press, Inc.

PRINTED IN THE UNITED STATES OF AMERICA

This book is dedicated to the loving memory of my mother Patricia Iona McKenzie-Dugal. A woman who taught me how to love and be loved. A mother who dedicated her life to her children and her creator - the greatest gift a parent can give. To my father Larry Dugal - all your sacrifices and hardwork is reflected in this book. It is your dedication to family that will be my lasting memory.

ACKNOWLEDGMENTS

I would like to thank the dynamic dual of my guidance guardians - Dori and Michelle. You have inspired me to reach beyond my dreams while keeping my feet on the ground. A special thanks goes to Carol my prayer warrior who has kept me on the proper path. Your faith in me has keep me believing in all that is good. A huge thanks goes to Liz because she welcomed me into a door that changed my life forever and gave me my first book of truth. I would also like to thank Christine for all her support and valued advice. To my brother Randy and sisters Kristine and Tabby - I want you to know that all we are and all we will become has been a gift from God. Live in the moment and always remember "Family First". Finally to my daughters Tessa and Brandi - the depth of my Love for you is as big as the sky and all the tea in China. You will pass in and out of many doorways but the most important door you can walk into is the last door in this book. This book has been written from God's heart to my hand - all credit goes to him.

TABLE OF CONTENTS

Acknowledgments		v
Chapter 1	The Arrival	1
Chapter 2	Finding the Moment	15
Chapter 3	Stealing and Sharing	27
Chapter 4	Agreeing With Yourself	39
Chapter 5	You are What You Eat	51
Chapter 6	Dream Catcher	69
Chapter 7	Web of Life	89
Chapter 8	The Calling	103
Chapter 9	The Climb	115

CHAPTER 1
THE ARRIVAL

"Looking for Lorax - call *lost-too*" was all the sign read that was posted on the old wooden telephone pole. It was filled with as many staples as a teacher's top drawer. What caught my eye was the telephone number: "lost too"? I asked myself, "Who is lost?" I am not. They are looking for someone and they are lost. A smile drew to my face as I thought, how can two people be lost at the same time? I also wondered, who was Lorax? Was it a dog or cat? Was it a family heirloom? Or was it a human? My mind played games with the sign for a few moments and then the real world came flashing back. A red sports car raced by and I was distracted by the long, slender-legged blonde crossing the street. I quickly walked toward her like a rabbit in heat. I fantasized our wedding night and how good-looking our children would be. The hop in my step was too slow and as quickly as she entered my life, she was through the door and into the shopping mall. Another lost beauty.

I refocused my thoughts to my purpose of this trip, to find an apartment. I walked past the shopping mall and entered the mouth of a weathered path that led into a vacant field. The pathway was winding and the tall grass surrounding this shortcut overflowed onto the dirt trail. The deeper I traveled, the more the path changed directions and the darker the path became. After a sharp right turn, I tripped over something half in the path, half in the field. I fell directly over this large mass of something. When I stood up a man yelled back at me, "It's not summer anymore. It's fall!" He began to laugh and asked me where I was going. I didn't reply. I stumbled to my feet to get a look at this man. He was sitting in the field and the first thing I noticed were his eyes. They were as blue as the clearest sky on a warm summer day. They were as deep as the ocean and as kind as the embracing branches of a large willow tree. He had a warm smile and his gray hair was neatly parted down the middle and pulled back from his face. He asked me again, "Where are you in such a rush to get to?" I softly told him that I was searching for a place to live.

For some reason my voice cracked as I was telling him and I felt strangely inferior to this man. My automatic defense mechanism rushed to get the upper hand and I asked him in a sarcastic tone, "Why are you lying in the middle of the field?" He simply replied in a soft whisper, "I am tired and taking a little nap." His voice quieted my testosterone rush and allowed my mind to settle enough to ask him if he knew where Apple Street was located. Slowly, he gathered his breath and rose to his feet. "I will show you if you would like." I nodded and he said, "Follow me." Together we picked up the path and slowly we walked through the field. After what seemed like hours of silence he asked me where I was from. I began to tell him and suddenly we were out of the field and at the end of the path. I noticed two large muscular men about thirty feet away looking directly at us. My voice quieted and we both stopped walking.

One of the men pointed at the old man. His friend pulled out a Polaroid picture from his front pocket. They both glanced down at the picture and by the time they looked up the old man had disappeared back into the field. The steroid-induced men began running straight at me. An adrenalin dump filled my arteries and veins, my feet felt like they where filled with cement, but somehow I turned myself around and I began running back into the field. I ran as fast as I could through the crooked pathway. One of the men in his deep voice screamed for me to stop running. My mind just kept saying "run" and I did until I tripped over something again. As I panicked to get up I felt something grab my arm and force me into the long slender grass. Another hand was placed on my mouth to silence me. I was confused. *Should I remain with this stranger or fight to get free and surrender to the muscle-bound hulks chasing me?* I was tired of running so I figured I would rest. The rustling of grass was replaced by the panting of the men approaching quickly. Louder their exhaled voices grew as they raced by us. Like lightning followed by thunder, quickly they disappeared out of sight and sound. I regained awareness of my situation and quickly turned my head around to see the old man.

To my surprise it was a woman. Her brown hair was covering most of her face and I gasped, "Who are you?" She replied by covering my mouth again and sharply stating to me that we are not out of the woods yet, they will be coming back. I immediately regained my personal space and stared at this woman. She stared back intently and I began to realize that this woman was not afraid; in fact, she was smiling with a whimsical look on her face. Her expression made me feel at ease with the situation. She had big brown eyes to match her hair and her cheeks and jawbone were strong yet sexy. My mind began to dance with the image of her naked body on a silk bed with the soft glow of a fireplace in the background. To my displeasure the voices of the bulk boys returning was beginning to filter the fresh air and this interrupted my beautiful dream. They were not huffing and puffing but talking. At first we could barely make out what they were saying but as they drew closer we could hear their words. The one said to the other, "If we don't find the old man then we will be placed in a hell like no other." The other man replied, "We are already in hell and the old man is the only way for us to get free."

Once again their words faded into the distance and my thoughts raced back to the old man. Where was the old man and why were these men looking for him? He seemed to be so nice and friendly.

Perhaps he was a serial killer and the two men were undercover police officers. Maybe I made a mistake. Suddenly the woman announced in a firm but polite voice, "No you did not make a mistake." With a queer look I asked her to repeat herself. She firmly repeated, "You didn't make a mistake; those men would have taken the old man." Startled by the woman's ability to read my thoughts I asked her how she knew what I was thinking. She said that it wasn't important right now and in a panicked tone she uttered that we should get out of here before nighttime draws upon the blades of this grass field. "What is the problem with this place at nighttime?" I asked. She just pierced me with her dark eyes and put her hand out for me to help her up. Being the gentleman I was, I jumped to my feet and took her hand into my hand.

As soon as my hand touched her silky smooth skin a vision flashed into my mind of demons floating like ghosts through the field. My grip on her hand released and she fell back on her hindquarters. "What is your problem?" she asked. Not to seem like a wimp I simply stated that I lost my grip and apologized. I grabbed her hand and lifted her up to her feet. The sun was settling on her back and the glow from behind her gave a silhouette of her shapely slender body. She was wearing tight-fitting jeans that accentuated her finely toned legs and her white T-shirt revealed the words "Looking for Lorax" in large black print. Puzzled at where I had seen that before, I asked her who Lorax was. She simply said it was a friend that was lost and turned to walk back down the path. As I walked behind her I couldn't help but notice how perfect her legs grew together and while I was in the midst of my trance she looked back over her shoulder and asked me if I wouldn't mind following something else.

Embarrassed by being caught, but not looking directly at her, I told her that God's creatures were meant to be enjoyed. She gave a half smile and turned her attention back to the path. As we approached the end of the path she slowed down to a halt. "What do we do now?" I asked. "We go home," she replied. I told her that I didn't have a home and that I was looking for an apartment on Apple Street. She quickly replied that Apple Street was not a good place to live and that the temptations to evil lurked about at every street corner. Surprised by her insights I asked her where a good place to live was. She said it is getting late and that I could crash at her house tonight and in the morning she would direct me to some nice places. The sun had just settled into its deep sleep and the moon was waking. The soft glow from the streetlights was just starting to form shadows on the objects below. She grasped my hand gently and tugged me in the direction of her house. I began to laugh with the thought of a woman rescuing me. She turned to me and without hesitation said, "Take help where you can; in life's journey you will need it." I immediately stopped laughing and tilted my head down toward the sidewalk confused but excited.

After a short walk, we arrived at her house. It was set back from the road and was surrounded by evergreen trees. She asked me if I was hungry as we climbed up the front stairs to her door. Starving! She nodded her head and opened the door. A flood of fresh scents filled my nostrils and as she turned the light on, the house revealed a warm welcoming. I immediately felt at home, like at grandmother's house. She walked into the kitchen and put a kettle of water on the stove. She told me to grab a seat. I picked up a chair that was located in the corner under a reading lamp and brought it to the kitchen. I asked her what she wanted to do with the chair. With a quarter smile she told me to relax in it. I was getting the feeling that she didn't appreciate my humor. I returned the chair to its rightful owner and sat on the sofa. "Tofu stir-fry okay with you?" she announced.

"Anything would be fine," I replied. She tended to her duties in the kitchen as I began to snoop around. On the mantle over her fireplace were pictures of many people; family members, I assumed. One of the pictures caught my eye, a man in a football uniform holding a young child in his arms. It looked like the old man but much younger.

He looked like a strong, athletic man, a receiver or a defensive back, I thought. Then I realized that I don't even know this woman's name. I quickly proclaimed that my name is Q and asked what her name was. She hesitated and then told me her name was Rose. "Rose is a pretty name," I replied, and without hesitation she asked me what Q stood for. "I'm not quite sure," I replied. She said that she liked my name. I thanked her and she announced that dinner was ready. We sat down at a dinner table that was dressed and ready for company. She poured me a cup of herbal tea and presented me with a plate filled with vegetables, tofu and rice. My palate was treated to a rare feast of flavors. Not much was said during dinner except my repeated compliments to the chef.

As we consumed the riches of the earth, my mind kept wandering back to the football picture and wondering if it was the old man. After, I foolishly volunteered to wash the dishes, which I was certain she would not let me do. I washed and she dried. I asked her about the football picture on the fireplace. She told me that it was her father and that she was the child. I asked her where her mother was and she popped her eyebrows up and said that she was taking the picture. Feeling a little stupid, I stopped asking questions until our chores were completed. We sat down in the living room to relax. "Why were you looking for a place on Apple Street?" she asked. "How much time do you have?" I replied. "Give me the Reader's Digest version," she pleaded.

"I moved here to go to university and my roommates and I were throwing a party to start the school year off with a bang," I told her. "To make a long story short, we burned down our house and all of my personal possessions went up in smoke."

"How did the house set fire?" she asked. "Well, it was a keg party and one of our house traditions was to light off fireworks at midnight," I answered. "Tom, the engineer in the house was in charge of lighting the magical stars and stripes. He just happened to trip while sipping his beer and kicked the pail filled with sand that was the base for lighting the fireworks. The pail tipped toward the house just as one of the fireworks was going off. It shot straight through the front window and the drapes caught on fire. Another roommate, Charlie, grabbed a bucket he thought was filled with water and threw it at the flames. A wicker chair in a blazing fire pit would have lasted longer than our house. The bucket was filled with sixty ounces of vodka, sixty ounces of gin and sixty ounces of tequila.

"I traditionally made this wicked punch for later in the night so we could 'howl at the moon.' Needless to say, by the time the fire department arrived, we were homeless peasants with beer breath and burnt eyebrows. I decided it was time to find a place without roommates and that is why I was going to Apple Street. A friend told me of a place that was vacant."

She asked me what I was taking in school and I told her that I was finishing my master's in Human Kinetics. I was starting to feel like I was doing all the talking and she was having all the enjoyment of listening. I abruptly finished my sentence and asked her what her T-shirt meant: Looking for Lorax. She told me that the many people in this community were trying to locate a person called Lorax. I asked her who Lorax was. She said that she had never met Lorax but she did know who Lorax was. She told me that the old man was a friend of hers and he was looking for Lorax.

Like a brick on the kneecap I remembered the sign on the telephone pole. I asked her if she had called the phone number "lost too." She told me that was the phone number of the old man and that he was in great danger because of his knowledge of Lorax. "I don't understand," I replied. "What does Lorax do?" She began to explain that Lorax was a protector of our earth. He had exposed corrupt governments that were poisoning our soil, water, and air all for power and money and then the phone rang. She excused herself and went into the kitchen. After a couple of minutes she returned with worry lines painted across her face.

I asked her if she was all right and she told me that the old man had just called and needed our help. I began to say something and she immediately started turning the lights off in the house. "We must go immediately," she said, and within the second we were out the door and on the street again. "Where are we going?" I asked.

"To the bridge by the field that we were in before," she replied. I began to get a little anxious and asked her if we had to cut through the field to get to the bridge. She sharply replied, "Never at night do you go into the field. Without daylight you can never find the path." I was fine with that; I really didn't want to see any flying demons anyway. We quickened our pace as we got closer to an old wooden bridge. It looked like the bridge connected two pieces of land across a valley that used to be filled with water. The old man was underneath the bridge when we arrived. Rose whistled three different tunes and the old man wandered out from beneath the bridge like a troll that had been there for years.

She ran to the old man and gently asked,

"Ismale, are you all right?" Ismale just smiled and embarrassed Rose with a big hug. As Ismale was hugging Rose he looked up at me and winked his right eye. "I see you brought me my friend," Ismale said to Rose. "You know him," Rose replied. "He is my apprentice," Ismale responded. "Excellent, he will make a fine student but just don't light this firecracker too early," Rose said. I chuckled with nervousness; whose apprentice is he talking about? I'm nobody's fool. I was wise enough to stay silent and listen to them talk. On our way back to Rose's house we were told that Ismale was being chased by government agents because he had information regarding the whereabouts of Lorax. Ismale told Rose that Lorax was somewhere in the mountains of British Columbia and that he must travel there as soon as possible to tell him something imperative. As we arrived at Rose's house, Ismale announced that he would see us in the morning. Rose gave him a brown paper bag with something in it. Ismale gave Rose a hug and a kiss on the cheek and then he turned to me and asked me to put out my hand. I thought that he was going to give me the brown paper bag and explain its contents. He slapped my hand and told me to get a good night's sleep because I was going to need it. Then he laughed and walked into the light on the street and out of sight.

I asked Rose, "What was he talking about, me being his apprentice? Is he crazy? I have my studies and my thesis to finish." Rose looked directly into my eyes with a frozen stare that seemed to last for an eternity and said, "Yeah, you're the one." "The one for what?" I asked. "It's in your eyes and your soul," she replied. Feeling uncomfortable I grabbed her hand and raised it to my heart. In a boyish grin, I asked her, "Are you in my heart?" She smiled openly and said, "Only in your dreams, lover boy." I shrugged my shoulders and we walked into her house.

I slept on the couch that night and had a wonderful sleep. When I woke Ismale was standing over me; he smiled and handed me some herbal tea and a bagel. I announced that I was only a coffee man in the morning. He ignored me and gave me the cup. "Drink this. It will help with your strength." I was too tired to fight so I drank the damm tea; it wasn't half bad. Sitting at the table was Rose. She was radiant and glowing like a fresh flower in spring. When she smiled at me and said good morning, I felt a warm rush intoxicate my senses; "Good tea," I responded. Ismale turned to Rose and asked her if everything was ready to go. She told him that everything was in the car and they were ready to go.

I quickly responded by asking if I could get a ride to the university. Ismale's voice grew serious and he began by saying that finding the path was only part of the journey; the awakening is what was needed next. I curiously looked at Ismale and said, "Old man, you're whacked out. What are you talking about?" He told me to take a seat at the kitchen table. On the table was a map of Canada. "We are here," he said as he pointed to Windsor, Ontario. "Here is where we are going. The distance between the two is your awakening." "You need to drink a coffee old man, so that you can awaken from your dream," I replied. "You are the one dreaming," the old man said. Rose gently placed her arm on my shoulder and whispered in my ear, "Travel with the old man and learn because he will set you free."

"Free from what? I am free and I'm also homeless but that is another matter." Rose stood up from her chair and softly grabbed my hand, as she did I saw a vision of a dove flying over the base of a river that led up into a mountain. As the bird climbed higher it changed appearances from a dove to a loon to a raven to an eagle. The climb was swift and direct and then the bird landed on top of a mountainside. The view down was awesome and unbelievable. It felt like heaven. From the bird's eye view, a flame of a fire could be seen straight across to the other side of the mountain and a person that was sitting by the fire waving his hand for me to come to him.

Rose let go of my hand and I stood up immediately and said, "So when do we leave?" Rose and Ismale began to laugh. I picked up the map and folded it. Ismale began to say goodbye to Rose and I interrupted his farewell by saying I was not going unless Rose was. Ismale turned to me and said that this journey is not for Rose but for me and that Rose will always be present, just not the way I now know. Rose hugged me and said, "Ismale is right. I will be with you always; you will feel me take your hand when you need it," and then she slipped a feather into my hand.

"What is this for?" I asked. "The answers will come later," she replied.

CHAPTER 2
FINDING THE MOMENT

We made our final goodbyes and headed out on the road. In the car I noticed the brown bag from the night before in the back seat. I asked Ismale what was in the bag. He told me to grab the bag from the back seat and open it up. To my surprise it was just a ring. "A simple copper ring, not even gold?" I asked. I asked Ismale, "What is with this cheap ring?" He told me if I complete my journey the ring would be mine. "A worthless ring, will be mine if I can get you to British Columbia," I chuckled with confidence. "I will get you to your destination and you can keep the worthless ring, old man."

The ride was quiet for about two hours and then the old man began to speak. His voice was soft but strong as he spoke. "I will teach you the ways of the energy circles and other truths of life. They will require your fullest attention and wits. You must trust your instincts and believe in the words that I speak. The lessons will come to you in many fashions and by many teachers. I will guide you but you must actively interact with your teachings and your surroundings. I will lead you to seven doors of knowledge that you must open, enter, and depart on your own; your own free will. I cannot join you for most of this journey but I will always be with you. Listen and speak equally. If anything listen more often than you speak. You will be tested in all realms of your being: physically, emotionally, and most importantly, spiritually. Practice your teachings and make it personal. Incorporate information into your life slowly, it will require a great amount of patience and effort."

"Hold on," I interrupted the old man, "What the hell are you talking about? What are the energy circles and where are these doors that I am to enter and leave?"

The old man pulled over to the side of the road. "Get out of the car," he insisted. "Why?" I asked. "Because I told you to," he replied. I looked at him momentarily and he smiled at me as if he was going to begin my training. I slipped out of the car and then the car wheels began to slide in the gravel as he drove off, leaving me at the side of the road. I cursed at him as he sped away. "You crazy old bat come back here I don't know where I am and I have no money." I watched as this yellow worn-out Comet drove out of sight. I began to walk in the same direction as the old man. I decided I would hitchhike to the next town, call a friend to pick me up, and get out of Dodge for good. Great adventure,

I said to myself, lost and alone with no one to talk to. I slammed my hand into my pocket and felt the feather that Rose had given me. I pulled it out and began to stroke the feathers calling out to Rose. Rose, rescue me, get me out of this place. Nothing happened. I chuckled to myself and then placed the feather in my hair. I will be a warrior on a spiritual journey, I joked to myself and kept on walking. My thumb must have been cursed because no one would pick me up. At least a dozen cars had passed by and the occupants all had this strange look on their faces. Finally, a man in a beat up pick-up rolled over to the side of the road and yelled to me, "Hey, chief, you need a ride?" Then it occurred to me: I still had the feather in my hair. No wonder no one would pick me up, I thought to myself. I grabbed the feather out of my hair and stuck it back into my pocket and I began jogging over to the truck.

As I grew closer to the truck, I realized that it was a teenage boy, probably around seventeen or eighteen, and he looked native. He had long, straight, dark hair and dark skin. I immediately thanked him for his kindness for picking me up. As I entered the bench seat of the truck, I noticed a guitar case behind his seat. Without hesitation he announced, "We tribal members must keep together." I turned to him to tell him that I wasn't a native and he began to laugh. "I know," was all he said.

"My name is Q," I proclaimed. "Quinn is my name," he said proudly. "Thanks for the lift Quinn," I said. "Where are you headed?" he asked. "I'm not sure," I replied. "To the next town, I guess." "You lost?" he inquired. "No, I was just . . . " I stopped not sure what to say. How do you explain to a total stranger that you were in a car with an old man that was taking you on a journey to discover energy circles and seven doors?

"I was with this old man and he took me as far as he could go and dropped me off. I just need a lift to the next town to call a friend to pick me up," I answered. "Not a problem," Quinn replied. "I am heading into town to get some supplies anyway." Silence fell over the truck for a spell. Quinn suddenly announced, "I'm on a journey." "A journey?" I asked. "Yeah, a journey to self-awareness and freedom from our domesticated culture," he announced. "Good for you," I said with a hint of sincerity and a cup of wonderment. "You are also on a journey," he replied. "How did you know?" I blurted out excitedly. "The old man told me," he replied. "What old man?" I asked with some reservation. "The old man in my dream," he replied. "He told me that I would find you and that I must tell you to live in the moment." "What are you talking about?" I said, confused. "You must silence your mind and put away the past and forget about the future. You must focus all your attention to the present and keep your mind alert to all around you. Listen attentively with your ears, smell fondly with your nose, and look fully with your eyes. As a thought enters your mind that is not from the present, calmly dismiss it and re-focus your energy to your surroundings. Do not fight with past or future thoughts. Your mind will be distracted with the struggle. Let the thought enter and pass peacefully by telling yourself to focus back on the present.

"We are here," he announced. "Where would you like me to drop you off?" "Anywhere is fine," I replied. "When you're lost any place is as good as the other," I said. "Only if you know what to look for," he replied. "I will let you off here." Thanks," I said gratefully. "How can I repay you?" "You already have," he said. Then he drove off.

I was standing on a sidewalk on the main street of a small town. The street shops were all dressed in autumn attire. It looked like a picture from that Norman Rockwell guy. My thoughts shifted back to what Quinn was saying: live in the moment, forget the past and the future. I quickly thought to myself that I have no future. I have no ride, no money, and no idea of where I am. A bench was located behind me so I thought I would sit for a spell. I rolled my neck around to get the kinks out and make a plan. I need to use a phone to call a friend, maybe Rose. I don't know Rose's number, I thought. My mind began to think about how I met Rose and the circumstance that we were in. I suddenly realized that I didn't ask Rose why she was in the field in the first place and why she was hiding in the grass. Was she being chased too? Maybe she is a spy for another government and just pretending to be Ismale's friend. Or maybe Ismale and Rose are partners and they are trying to capture me for some reason. "Stop," I said to myself. "Focus on the present moment." My eyes surveyed the street. Across the street was a pawnshop. Perhaps the owner will let me use his phone, I said to myself. I walked across the street and my thoughts raced about where Rose was and what she was doing. I didn't realize that a car was heading right for me. At the last minute I jumped out of its way. The angry man shot me the finger as he passed by. A lesson, I said to myself; stay in the moment. I entered the pawnshop and a wiry old man was behind the counter. His face was worn from all his years of bartering with people. He smiled when our eyes met and asked me how I was doing. "Just great," I replied. "I was wondering if I may use your phone." "I have no phone," the man said.

"Sorry but there is a pay phone down the block at the variety store." I was about to leave and then a painting of a dove in full flight caught my eye. The man noticed and told me that he had a thing for doves. "They are creatures that represent honesty and love," he explained. I pulled the feather out of my pocket and asked him if he knew what the feather was from. "Let me see it," he replied. I passed it to him and he quickly announced that it was a dove's feather. "What is it worth to you?" I asked. He replied, "It was probably worth more to you than to me. You are the one carrying it around; it must have some meaning to you." I told him that it did. "It was given to me by a very lovely girl," I replied. "But I need money," I pleaded. He surveyed the feather again and told me that he would give me a loonie for it. "A loonie," I replied in anger. "It is just a worthless feather," the man stated. "A loonie is a great price for this feather." I thought about it for a second and realized that a loonie for a feather was a great deal and it would give me change to make four separate phone calls. "I will take it," I said. "Great," he replied. As I was walking out the door a phone rang from inside; I shook my head and smiled.

My thoughts began to plan my next sequence of events; I would cash in the loonie at the store and maybe buy some penny candies and use the rest for calls. Just as I approached the variety store I heard a car beeping its horn. I turned to look and it was the old man. "Get in," he shouted. "Go to hell," I said in defense. "I'm not the one in hell. You are and this car is your only salvation you stupid poor bastard," he replied. He smiled at me and my legs moved to him without my knowledge. Before I knew it, I was back in the car and we were driving out of town. "How was your first lesson?" he asked. "Great lesson," I replied. "You left me stranded with no money and no ride." "You made it to town okay, didn't you?" he said with a curious tone. I thought for a minute and realized that I had stepped into my first door. "I was picked up by an Indian boy named Quinn and he said that he talked to you in his dreams." "He didn't talk to me," the old man replied. "He must have been talking about another guide." "What did he have to say?" Ismale asked. "He told me to live in the moment and forget the past or the future. He told me to smell, hear, and see everything around me." "He forgot to tell you about taste and touch," Ismale replied with a sarcastic laugh. "Did it work?" he asked. "When I was on the bench and I cleared my mind I saw a pawnshop. I sold my feather for a loonie." "You ripped him off," Ismale said jokingly. "I guess so," I replied.

"Listen closely to what I am about to say," Ismale said with the most serious tone. "Living in the present is the only way to clear the mind to accept the signs you will need on your journey. The energy that the mind consumes in the past and in the future will dominate its ability to communicate at a higher plane because it is not in the present moment." I interrupted to ask him what was wrong with learning from our past and planning our future. "Nothing is wrong with those activities as long as they don't consume the mind. I will ask you a simple question. Have you ever made a mistake in your life?" "Yes, many," I replied curiously. "Have you ever played out that mistake over and over in your head and wish you could take back that moment?" "Yes, that is what all humans do," I replied. "We feel guilt and regrets sometimes for our actions," Ismale said. "It is only normal for humans to feel this way. Guilt, shame, regret, remorse, and fear all dominate time frames that we can no longer control," Ismale said.

"If we can't live in this moment, the time that we can control...how can we expect to live and control the unknown moments, the ones that lie ahead...and the past moments . . . the ones lost in time?" Ismale said. "That makes sense to me but we need to plan for the future," I replied. "You're right," Ismale said. "But the future is a time and place yet explored. Unfortunately, humans obsess about living in images of untold story. Planning ahead is far different from living ahead. Humans have the capacity to plan outcomes and strategically plan events. This ability should not be filled with fear and anxiety. If it is, then it has been given a breath of life and it becomes a part of our present life. Once we begin to live ahead we lose the connection with the current moment of our consciousness and therefore the collective consciousness." "What is the collective consciousness?" I asked. "It is the consciousness of all living beings on this planet," he said. "In particular, it is the higher level of communication that we as humans are entering. An awakening of our sense that we all share this planet is emerging and with it is also the understanding that all our collective thoughts and dreams are working together. I will explain more later," he exclaimed.

"Fear often dominates the unknown of the future. It becomes a creature of demons that consumes the mind." "Wait a minute," I said. "When I touched Rose's hand in the field after she told me not to go there after dark, I saw demons floating across the grass." "Fear is a product of not being able to see your path when you look too far ahead. Fear is our way of giving into the control we could have on our life," he explained.

"I see what you are saying about the future but we need to learn from the mistakes we made in the past. How will we ever stop making the same mistake if we ignore our history?" I asked. "Learning from past mistakes is far different than living in your past mistakes. We fail in our awareness of the present when our mind's energy is filled with past memories. We punish ourselves for the past more than any other species on this planet. We are creatures that will punish a mistake over and over. The past failures become weapons to slay the energy of others. When we compete for energy, we throw daggers of past mistakes on our consciousness. We will use blame and guilt to steal the energy from other humans, even the ones we love the most," he replied.

"More dangerous than this is when a person self-induces this pain," he continued. "Living in regret and remorse for past mistakes will weaken the mind from accepting anything from the present. A perceived punishment is inflicted into our consciousness to pay for past mistakes. How many times have you said to yourself, "I deserve that for whatever reason." We place our minds in a prison as payment for past indiscretions. The consumption of this energy drains the mind and in some cases it can be lethal. The past is part of life but not the living part. It has no room in our present life.

"Living in the past and future is also an energy flow that blocks the collective consciousness from moving forward. We play back the tapes of the day and prey upon the mistakes we make. We punish ourselves with thoughts of shame, guilt, and fear to replace acceptance and the right to enjoy each living moment. Energy from the past and future are similar because they both have the ability to block energy needed for growth," Ismale said. "What makes us live in the past and dream about the future?" I asked. "It is a product of our upbringing," he answered. "We are truly products of our environment and the homes that we lived in. Some of us were nurtured in homes filled with guilt and fear. Our parents were our caregivers and they were only doing what was done to them. They were victims to energy flow issues because their parents used guilt, fear, shame, regret as teaching tools to shape behavior. We are domesticated by the emotions that we share. If the emotions are filled with negative energy then the responding flow of energy will be the same." "I don't understand what you mean by the emotional energy flow," I stated. "You will in time because that is your next doorway of information," he said.

We pulled in to a motel on the side of the road called Shady Hills. We entered the office and a middle-aged lady greeted us with an amazing smile and a twinkle in her eyes. "What can I do for you gentlemen?" she asked. Ismale asked for a room for the night. They exchanged pleasantries while I looked around.

On the wall behind the counter was a motto framed in a unique birchwood design. It read:

> Fear not the future...it is unknown
> Forget the past...it is foreknown
> Forgive the present...it is what we need
> to know
> Lorax

The lady caught my eye as I was reading the motto; she smiled and nodded her head knowingly. I smiled and nodded my head in acceptance. We walked back to the car and Ismale opened the trunk to retrieve some bags. He tossed me a duffle bag and told me everything that I would need was in this bag. I asked, "Even a toothbrush?" "Even toe clippers," he replied. I told Ismale that I was starving. He opened a basket that was filled with sandwiches, nuts, fruit, and raw vegetables. "Go nuts," he said. "Where's the beef?" I asked. "In the cows, you idiot," he replied. "Why don't you eat meat?" I asked. "It's simple," he stated. "All energy that we consume from has a role. Think of your body as the motor to a car and the food the gas. If you put bad fuel into the car you will get poor performance. The same holds true for your body. It will be explained later but now it is time to sleep."

With that he turned out the night table light on his side of the bed and he fell asleep within seconds. I stayed up and pigged out on the peanut butter and jelly sandwiches until I passed out.

CHAPTER 3
STEALING AND SHARING

Ismale woke me up by tearing the drapes open to reveal the blinding sun. "Good morning sunshine," I said sarcastically. "Did you sleep well?" Ismale asked. "Another great sleep," I said. "Except for this feeling like somebody was watching me sleep. I actually woke up in the middle of the night to see if anyone else was in the room." "Perhaps there is someone watching over you," Ismale said. I laughed if off but I strongly felt the presence of something else. "Gather your stuff and let's get going," he said. He tossed me an apple and we were out the door. We traveled for about an hour with silence ringing in my ear. "Can we put the radio on?" I asked, breaking the silence. "Concentrate on the present and focus in on your surroundings," Ismale said. "You are in training and you must practice." I did for the next couple of hours. It was amazing what your eyes can see when your mind is in the present. The trees were proud and majestic. The birds were playful and free. The sun seemed to tickle the earth. I was astonished with the story I was seeing for the first time.

We were entering a city when all of a sudden, sirens were blasting from behind us. Ismale looked into his rear-view mirror and realized that it was us that they wanted. He pulled over to the soft shoulder and rolled down his window to greet the officer. "Excuse me," the officer said. "May I see your driver's license and insurance?" "What is the problem?" Ismale inquired. "This car has been reported stolen," the police officer said. "Impossible," Ismale replied. "My friend Rose is the owner and she is lending it to me." The officer took Ismale's information and walked back to his car. "Ismale, is this Rose's car?" I asked. "I believe it is," Ismale responded.

The officer returned and informed Ismale that he must follow him to the station to straighten this out. Ismale agreed and then he turned to me and pointed to a diner down the street. "I will meet you there once I straighten this out," he said. "I will go with you," I replied. "You go and get yourself something to eat and I will be right back," Ismale responded. I didn't hesitate at the thought of getting a good greasy meal. "See you soon," I said as I stepped out of the car. I began to walk toward the diner when I realized that all I had to my name was the loonie from the pawnshop. "Oh well, at least I could get a hot cup of Joe," I thought.

In fact, it wasn't Joe but Charley who was my waitress; at least that's what it said on her name tag.

LOOKING FOR LORAX · 29

The breakfast crowd was gone and the lunch crew hadn't yet arrived. I sat down in a booth near the window so that I could see Ismale when he arrived. Charley was a middle-aged waitress with her hair in a bun and wearing a white uniform looking like a nurse. She took one look at me and said, "Boy you look hungry." "I am," I cried. "What can I get you, darling?" she asked. "I only have a loonie," I stated. "So I will just have your finest cup of coffee." "You need more than coffee," she said. "I will fix you up in a jiffy." She walked away but before she did she glanced over at the table adjacent to me. I looked over to see what she was looking at. A man was scolding his young son for spilling his water on the table. The mother was feverously trying to wipe up the mess and their other child was laughing.

Moments later Charley arrived back at my booth with a plate full of food and a hot cup of coffee. "I don't have enough money to pay for this," I exclaimed. "I won't charge you if you keep me company while I take my break." "Not a problem," I said with excitement. Charley sat down and asked me all the usual introductory questions, where I was from, what my name was and where was I going. She made me feel at ease and she seemed very open-minded. So I told her, "I was on my way to British Columbia and I was traveling with an old man that was teaching me about energy." "What are the two most important things in our life?" she asked. "I don't know what you mean," I said. "What makes us do what we do?" "Money and a desire to be rich and famous," I said. "Not even close," she said with the white of her teeth.

"Since the beginning of time, man has been striving for two ultimate goals in life: love and happiness. These two common bonds are the threads that bind all living creatures on our planet. The fallout to our society is the difficulty achieving these elements in our daily life. Humans respond to situations in life by either stealing energy or sharing it. Most people are not aware of what they do and why they do it. We pattern our energy exchanges early in life and we truly are a product of our environment. Energy is taught in the home and transferred to the child by repeated behavior. A child will most certainly pattern the energy givers that they are in most contact with. A child will respond to situations in the same manner that their parents respond. It becomes their energy culture."

She paused to take a sip of her tea. I interrupted and asked her, "What is energy culture?" "For example, a child brought up in a home that has been pre-occupied by yelling and screaming to exchange energy will produce a child that will react to situations by yelling and screaming," she said. "Take the example that just occurred in here. The child spilled his water. The reaction from the parents was violent. One parent became visibly upset and scolded the child. The other parent slapped him on the hand to teach him not to do it again. The child's energy is drained because it has been stolen from his parent. That same child now has to replace energy stolen, so he kicks his brother who was laughing at him. Energy exchange of stealing has been reinforced and copied."

"Children fight all the time," I said. "Why do

they fight?" Charley asked. "Because they get on each other's nerves," I said. "There is always a reason why and it all revolves around energy," Charley said. "Close your eyes," she added. "Now think of someone that makes you happy." "Okay what now?" I asked. "Ask yourself why that person makes you happy, think in terms of energy flow." "Ah, ah..." I said. "But can I open my eyes now?" "Only if you are willing to see differently," Charley said. I opened my eyes and looked at Charley, who was grinning from ear to ear. "Okay," I said. "If people steal energy, then the energy they steal will drain the person that they stole the energy from, right?" "Yes, you are right but you must also be aware that any energy that is gained by stealing is only temporary energy. As quickly as it is stolen, it is lost and must be replaced. The mechanics of stealing energy is complicated and not readily understood. Sometimes by understanding how to share energy, it makes a greater awareness of why we steal energy."

"How do we share energy?" I asked. "Sharing energy is a mutual energy exchange that is lasting and fulfilling," Charley said. "When humans share energy, they not only keep a balance of their energy but also have the ability to share this energy with others. It is similar to the energy that is gained from the sun. It is continuous and plentiful. If it is passed on, it not only grows as an energy source but it becomes the sole energy source. All other sources realize its benefits and want its results. Regardless of man's passion for power, money, and materialistic goods, our basic instinct from an infant is to be loved and be happy. Why did you choose that person?" "Well, my grandmother is kind, doesn't judge me, and makes me laugh," I said. "She doesn't steal your energy, does she?" Charley said. "No, she is always positive and has a great outlook on life." "People who know how to share energy usually know how to enjoy each moment of life. They rarely spend too much time outside of the here and now."

"Charley, your break is over!" someone yelled from the kitchen. "Got to go," she said. "How can I pay you?" I asked. "By sharing energy with others, because the more people share the less people will steal." I pulled out my loonie from my pocket and presented it to Charley. "I would like to share this with you," I said. "I accept," she proclaimed. Charley pulled out a pen from her pouch and said that she wanted to share this with me. I thanked her and she walked away.

Just as I was about to sit back down, Ismale arrived out of nowhere and instructed me to get myself in gear because we had to go. I put the pen in my pocket and into the car I went. "Have you been spying on me?" I asked Ismale. "I don't have time for games like that, kid," he said with a grin. "What happened at the police station?" I asked. "I found out that the government agents picked up Rose and they were the ones that put out the A.P.B. on the car." "Is Rose okay?" I asked. "She is fine but now they know where we are. We must be careful from this point forward. We must be careful about whom we talk to and where we go. I think we will travel on the back roads for the next couple of days to stay out of sight."

Ismale then asked me how my food was. "It was very interesting," I said. "What did you learn?" he asked. "I learned about sharing and stealing energy by a woman named Charley. I understand that we are a product of our environment but we have two different sources, mom and dad, that we get energy from that help shape our energy culture. Each parent will bring different energy flow patterns." "You are right," Ismale said. "But since you were an infant the pattern of your energy flow was being imprinted into your consciousness by both parents. You have to understand your parents' home life to understand how they raised you. Knowing how they were raised will help you understand the way they raised you. For example, a traditional family had two parents: each parent will bring with them their own pattern for energy exchange. Back in the day divorces and separations were rare because they were not socially accepted. Parents would live together out of obligation and not always love because of the social condition at the time. The commitment to stay together without love was a breeding ground for stealing energy. Without love there cannot be happiness and the hollow spirits that roamed the halls of these homes made for very poor energy exchanges.

"Anger and resentment filled the air and the only mechanism for dealing with it was to steal. The majority of parenting skills practiced in the past were used to steal energy to produce desired behavior. Corporal punishment was the order of the day. Discipline and conformity were prized assets for most parents and the mechanism for that behavior was physical discipline. The children subjected to that style of parenting have continued with that type of parenting or have separated from that cycle of abuse and have become aware of other measures to discipline, sharing. Why do you think that over 50 percent of marriages fail? The reason is simple. They don't want to exist in a home life that they were raised in, but unfortunately people marry the same energy people as their parents.

"Back then a child received a blended pattern of energy exchange from their parents," he continued. "One parent, usually the father, would discipline and the mother would nurture. But in today's society that pattern has been broken somewhat because both parents work. Other caregivers are given the responsibility to help shape and form energy patterns. They may spend the majority of their time with a grandparent or an aunt. The child will now assume energy flow patterns from those sources. Nevertheless, a child is a product of his or her environment and the old saying that an apple doesn't fall far from the tree is totally relevant. The energy flow of a child and a caregiver is easily understood by their ability to communicate in life's daily situations. The simple things in life, such as spilled milk or mud on the floor, become the building blocks to a lifetime of energy exchanges. If the process to resolve these little annoyances is by stealing energy then there is a good chance that the child will demonstrate the same strategies in similar situations.

Ismale went on, "Stealing energy comes in

many forms and varying degrees of intensity. Humans will play out many roles, called dramas, to receive energy. They will act out in anger or become aloof or play the 'poor me.' All strategies developed to receive energy from the caregiver. The most volatile is physical. The feelings of guilt and remorse usually follow a physical episode. The next step in this energy flow is to give energy back. The cycle will continue for as long as both partners allow it to. One will hit the other, stealing energy from that person and then the guilt and regret sets in and then they will give energy back. They will buy them something nice and treat them with attention given to royalty. They share their source of regret and beg for forgiveness, this giving of energy is taken from the source that is hollow and empty. It is taken to complete the cycle of stealing energy and temporarily fulfilling the needs of being loved and happy."

"I don't understand," I said. "It is wrong for me to give energy to the people I love?" I asked. "Givers and takers of energy are the direct relatives of pure stealers of energy," he replied. "Therefore, it can never be termed sharing energy. Givers and takers fulfill their energy exchanges by the feeling of guilt, regret, shame, and remorse. The most powerful of all is guilt. It has the ability to deplete a person's total energy source, leaving them vulnerable to stealing more energy. Guilt is associated with every negative energy source known to man. Guilty people try to give away their energy and if it is not accepted by anyone, it often results in self-deprivation acts and in extreme cases, suicide. We carry guilt like a banner to shield us from the ultimate truth, our inability to be loved and feel happy. It is often alcoholics' and drug abusers' final refuge."

"How do we help these people?" I asked with sadness. "A human full of guilt is a fragile human," he said. "They hang on to this feeling, energy source, to represent their past failures in life. Failures they have artificially injected by poor energy sources. They are usually victims to a home life of stolen energy and negative consequences. No human chooses to be in an environment that is full of unhealthy energy but unfortunately we become products of it. As their awareness increases about energy and its dynamics, so will their ability to understand and accept the reality of their misfortunes. As humans we can only control one thing and one thing only, ourselves. Humans will say and do what they please. Unfortunately we can only truly control our own actions and our own thoughts. Guilt is a burden when one doesn't recognize its ugly face. Guilt is dissolved when a human begins to accept the only realities of life: taxes, death, and the command of one's own destiny."

"Wow...that was a lot," I said. "Don't try to absorb it all at once," Ismale said. "Incorporate it slowly into your mind and use your life experiences as a backdrop to see it. Once you make sense of it yourself then try to look for it in your present surrounding. Observe the behaviors of others in each waking moment to gain a greater understanding. Enough sharing for one day, we must find a place to camp tonight. We are going to stay clear of motels and use the tent I brought to sleep at night." Ismale brought us to a camping ground for the night. We set up camp quickly and had a bite to eat before retiring to our tent. Before we fell asleep I asked Ismale two questions that had been lingering in my head.

"Who is Rose?" I asked curiously. "What do you want to know?" Ismale replied. "Tell me about her likes and dislikes, what she does for a living, her favorite color, her favorite food, what movies she likes," I said. "She is a simple woman with a great amount of talents and gifts," Ismale said. "She doesn't like dishonest people and she doesn't like people who value making green over being green. Rose was raised in a family of environmental freaks; and I mean that in a good way. She knows firsthand about the corruption of governments and corporations when dealing with the treatment of our environment. Her father has been battling with these people since she was born. She has a gift of prophesy and she has powerful visions. Her heart is open but always on guard. She knows how to love but she will only love those that invest the time to get to know her. She loves sports and she is a very good athlete. She played varsity basketball, volleyball, and track, like her father. Her mother has been involved with Greenpeace for a very long time but now she spends most of her time with the organization PETA. My advice to you, young man, is to be yourself and not fake who you are. Rose is very intelligent and she will see right through you. The night you slept over at her house, she told me that she felt a strong energy flow from you and she knew that you were going to be important to Lorax. She told me that she felt that your spirit was fighting to be revealed but it was being hidden because of some skeletons in your closet." Ismale took a breath. "But did she say that she liked me?" I asked sarcastically. "Like you? You're just a young child trying to find his blankie," Ismale said, laughing.

"Why don't you ever call me by my first name?" I asked. "You haven't earned the right of your name yet," Ismale said. "I don't even know what my name stands for," I said. "You are learning and still a student. When you graduate and become a teacher, I will address you accordingly. Now try and get some sleep. Tomorrow we have a busy day." "Goodnight Ismale," I said. "Goodnight my Jedi student," he said with a chuckle. As I settled into my sleep, I realized that I walked through my second door, the door at the diner.

A truck door and a diner door! Moving and eating, I thought to myself. Nomads like in the beginning of time. Moving from place to place and discovering all of God's gifts, I thought. I wondered to myself if this journey would help me better understand myself. I wonder if it will bring me closer to Rose. I wonder if it will help me understand God's plan for my life. I wonder...

CHAPTER 4
AGREEING WITH YOURSELF

We woke early with the dew still clinging to the grass. We packed our things quickly and were on the road in no time. "Today we must find a computer, so that we can get a hold of Rose," Ismale said. "Why don't we call her?" I asked. "I don't trust the phones anymore, we must secure our location," he replied. "Okay," I said. We traveled into a small town and stopped in front of a library. "We will stop here for a while," Ismale said. "I will go and get some more supplies and return later in the afternoon." "What do you want me to do in the meantime?" I asked. "Go into the library and find something to read," Ismale said. "What?" I asked. "Think of your lessons and go from there," he said, irritated. Ismale drove away and left me on the doorsteps of the library. I walked up to the door and reached out to grasp the large wooden handle. It took a great amount of effort to open the doors. I walked in and sat down at a table. I didn't have any idea what I should read. I opened my eyes and my mind to my surroundings. I saw a newspaper rack with papers from different cities. I will get a newspaper, I thought to myself. I will catch up on what is going on in this world. I picked up a local paper and was flipping through the paper when I came upon an advertisement. It was entitled, AGREEING WITH YOUR SELF WORKSHOP. It was set for that day's date and was being held in a seminar room at the library at 9 a.m.

I adjusted myself in my seat to find a clock and realized that it was 9:15 a.m. I also realized that no one was at the front counter or in the library at all. I got up to find out where the seminar room was. I saw a sign for the seminar room pointing to the back of the library. I nervously walked to the seminar room door that separated those inside from me. I didn't want to interrupt the workshop but I felt compelled to open the door and walk in. As I did, a man from behind me said, "Welcome, go right in." Spooked from his arrival, I thanked him and walked in. I wondered where he had come from. As I made my way through the doors I saw a small group of four people sitting around an oval table. They all looked up at me. The man from the hallway asked me to take a seat next to him.

Feeling awkward, I sat down. "My name is Leroy," he announced. "What is your name?" he asked. "I am Q," I said. "I am not sure why I am here. I saw the advertisement in the paper so I decided to come." I tried to defend and explain my reasoning for being there but it didn't seem to matter. Leroy asked the group members to introduce themselves and he gestured to his right. "Hi! I am Shannon and this is my ten–year-old grandchild." "Hi! My name is Maria," the girl said as she hugged her Winnie the Pooh doll. "Hello! My name is Todd," the next person said in a very humble voice. "Hi everyone my name is R...for Randy," another said, filled with fire in his tongue. "Just kidding," he said while looking at me. "I am Leroy and I will be guiding this workshop entitled 'Agreeing with Your Self.' If I may start. The purpose of this workshop is to find a better awareness of ourselves and our surroundings. Before we can accept the things in and around our lives we must first accept who we are and what our role is in this life. I will describe what my belief system is to begin. Each of us has our own perspective on life and how we should live it. Your role as active participants is to engage in these philosophies and customize them to shape the world that you want to live in. The mystical natures of Taoism and Toltec language will be discussed but not until we learn a little more about our new friend Q."

Surprised at my inclusion in this discussion, I asked Leroy what he wanted me to say. "What brings you here to this moment?" he asked. I looked around the room and felt at home. "I am here as part of my travels to British Columbia." "That is where you are going, but why are you here?" Leroy asked. "I am on a journey to find seven doorways," I explained. "Excellent," Leroy replied. "Thank you for sharing openly." Todd smiled generously at me to make me feel more comfortable for disclosing my little secret. "We are all here for a variety of reasons, so I will ask Shannon to share first," Leroy announced.

"Vinegar taster, cobblestone maker, uncarved block show me the way", she said in a riddle. She continued, "Busy Backston, sitting back and relaxing, trying to eat pie each day." Totally confused, I blurted out, "What you are talking about?" "The ways of Taoism written in a song," she said. "Oh!" I said. "I will try and explain," she said. She asked me, "If you dipped your finger in vinegar and tasted it, what would it taste like?" "It would be sour and bitter," I said.

"But why is it sour and bitter?" she replied. "Because the ingredients in it make the tongue receptors tell us it is sour," I answered. "The vinegar taster in life is viewed from many perspectives," she said. "What if I told you that the vinegar was actually sweet?" "I would say you spiked it with something," I said. "From the Taoist point of view, interference from the unappreciated mind makes it bitter and sour," she replied. "Life itself is what you make of it. Think of vinegar like life: you have the choice to taste what you like."

"I taste sour," I said. "It is your choice," she said. "But wouldn't it be great if it was sweet as honey?" She continued, "Cobblestone maker and the uncarved block are working together. The uncarved block represents things in their original state: simply containing power and being. The uncarved block represents a life that is childlike and fun. The cobblestone maker is man and in his haste, he wants to change and shape all the objects around him without taking the time to appreciate the beauty of their natural state. If the cobblestone maker understands the uncarved block then he understands the way." "What way?" I said. "The way to serenity and happiness," she replied. "Finally, the Busy Backston, sitting back and relaxing, trying to eat pie each day, represents a contradiction in terms. Man is so busy that he can't purely enjoy sitting back and relaxing, enjoying the fruits of his labor. The mind fast forwards ahead in one minute and in the next minute it is rewinding to play out the last day's events. For many the mind doesn't have the ability to enjoy the simple things such as an apple pie. The mind is never quiet enough to live in the moment and sit and relax. To do is easy, not to do is the challenge," she said.

She turned to her grandchild. "Am I right, honey?" "Pooh says you're just fine, Grandma," she replied. "Thank you," Leroy said. "Does anyone else have anything to say?" Todd cleared his voice. "I agree with Shannon, most of our time is spent in a place we are not. Our understanding of ourselves must agree with who we are and what we want to be. What I am trying to say is that if our consciousness is being contradicted by our actions then those struggles in our mind dominate our existence. We dream constantly of the way we believe things should be but we fail in our ability to change these things. The warrior in us is hidden in the shadows of our fears. We continually tell ourselves that we can make changes, but few do." "Why?" I asked. "What are we afraid of?"

Todd looked directly at Leroy. "It is our

agreements with our self that blocks the way," Leroy said. "We have been programmed by mother culture about the way we should be and how we should behave. The Toltec Book of Wisdom tells us that our belief systems are domesticated before we even have a chance to make decisions ourselves. As children we are told that this is a book." Leroy held up a book. "We believe it to be a book so we make an agreement with ourselves that it is a book. We are conditioned to make thousands of agreements about many things in life and when we make those agreements we learn how to live and dream. We train our children the same way that we would train and domesticate any other species on this planet. We use systems of punishments and rewards. We punish unwanted behaviors and reward desired behavior. The rewards feel good, so we keep doing what others want in order to get the reward! In turn, we become a copy of our caregivers' beliefs.

"As we become more domesticated we will make a book of internal laws that solidify our agreements with ourselves. We bind ourselves to these laws. We will also become the judge and jury when we break these laws. We will punish ourselves with guilt and shame, emotions that will be used as deterrents for making further disagreements with the book of laws that we created. We will carry past mistakes with us to remind us of our violations to the book.

"Todd, this is why it is so difficult to make changes in our lives according to the Toltec philosophy," Leroy said. "We are conditioned by our agreements within our consciousness. Our visions and dreams have been lost in the way we are domesticated."

Suddenly, Randy rose to his feet and announced that he was leaving. "I have no clue what any of you are saying. You all seem like really nice people but I thought that this was about saying yes to being me. Agreeing with the person I am and not worrying about what anyone else thinks of me!" "You are right, you're totally right," Leroy said. "I am!" Randy said in disbelief. "Agreeing with ourselves is being aware of who you are and what you are doing; but more importantly, why we are doing what we do," Leroy said. "That is what this workshop is about, Randy, trying to figure out why you do what you do in life. There is a reason for everything that we do, whether we realize it or not. But to make changes we must be aware of why we do the things we do."

"Cool!" Randy exclaimed as he sat back down. "I was just introduced to the understanding of sharing and stealing energy by a waitress I met," I said. "She explained to me that we behave in certain ways because of our energy culture. We will gain energy to feel loved and be in a state of happiness. The mechanisms to receive energy come from stealing energy and sharing energy. Sharing energy being the preferred way of receiving energy." "What do you mean?" Shannon asked. "As humans we want to be loved and be happy," I said. "But we must find the energy to achieve these two goals. Most humans are conditioned to steal energy because of the way they were brought up. For example, how did your parents handle life's little annoyances? Spilled milk, toothpaste cap left off, bread crumbs on the counter. If they yelled and screamed or even used physical punishment then they were stealing your energy. The cycle of stealing energy leads to more stealing. The emptiness you feel after someone steals energy must be replaced in order to create balance. Have you ever been in an argument and felt totally drained? How did you get your energy back?"

"I would yell at my sister," Randy announced. "Once you yelled at your sister, how did you feel?" I asked. "I felt great," Randy replied. "How long did it last?" I asked. Randy thought to himself for a few seconds. "Not long enough, so I would yell at her again."

"Your parents would steal energy from you, you would steal energy from your sister," I said. "And your sister would have her own way to steal and replace her lost energy. When you steal energy it is a temporary boost to your energy supply. It doesn't last because we want to make room for more lasting energy, love, and happiness. Sharing energy is the purest form of gaining lasting energy, love and happiness. Sharing energy is a mutual exchange of energy that is lasting and fulfilling. Sharing energy doesn't bruise our ego or shatter others. It doesn't judge or intentionally try to hurt others. People who share energy don't blame or point fingers. They just appreciate who you are and who they are."

"I have an uncle like that," Randy said. "He makes me feel good about myself when I am with him. He doesn't criticize my mistakes or make fun of the way I dress. I like to dress like a cowboy sometimes," he joked. "He listens to me and shares his life stories with me. I always walk away feeling great when I'm with him."

"Those are the people we must include in our lives," Leroy said. "They are positive people that rarely trouble themselves with thought of the past and worries of the future. They share in the moment and give their fullest attention to who they are sharing their time with. A person that knows how to share understands that to be fully present with someone that they must be totally absent of themselves."

Todd spoke up, "We are all sharing now. It is a wonderful feeling to allow our inner-person to be revealed without being judged or embarrassed." "You can feel a heightened energy flow," Shannon said. "I feel it too," Randy replied. "We all do," Leroy said. "When we break down the barriers of our life, we digest a greater understanding of ourselves and the people around us." Leroy looked up at the clock. "Unfortunately, our time is up and we must depart." We all said goodbye by hugging each other. It was an awesome feeling. As I walked into the main corridor of the library, I could see Ismale on a computer. I walked up to him and asked him if he had Rose online. "She is," he said. "May I say something to her?" I asked. "Sure, give me a minute," he replied. I was trying to think of something full of wisdom and insight to say to her and then I decided to let it go.

"Here you go," Ismale said. I began typing.

Hello Rose, How are you doing? I am enjoying my lessons and learning a great deal. I wish you were here! I know in my heart we will be together again.
See you soon, Q.

"We must go," Ismale said. I sent off the e-mail and we headed out the door. As we were driving I asked Ismale if Rose had sent him any information. "Yes, she did," he said. "We must get rid of the car as soon as possible and travel by train to our next destination." "What is wrong with the car?" I asked. "It is still in the system as being stolen. If we are caught in it we will be brought directly to jail. Because we don't have a 'get out of jail free' card, we must find another mode of transportation," he said with a smile. "Quit joking," I said. "Why is the car still registered as stolen?" "The people who want to find us will stop at nothing to stop us from reaching our destiny," he replied.

We stopped talking long enough for me to remember my time in the seminar room. "How was your day?" Ismale asked. "It was great," I replied. "I learned a little about Toltec and Taoist philosophies." "Can you incorporate them into your life?" Ismale asked. "I believe so," I said.

"We will see," Ismale responded. "What was your greatest insight that you learned?" Ismale asked, curiously. "I learned that we must accept things as they are. A person must not be too quick to change someone or something. God intended things a certain way and it is that way for a reason." "Not bad, my little protégé", Ismale replied sarcastically.

Ismale pulled the car into a vacant lot adjacent to a train station. "We will leave the car here," he said. "What are we going to do now?" I asked. He pointed toward the station. "We will take the choo-choo train." "Okay," I replied. Ismale went in and purchased the ticket as I stayed out by the train tracks. It was an old-time train station with one track going out and one coming in. The station master was dressed in his royal blue uniform standing proud and majestic. He pulled out his pocket watch almost as to announce that the train would be arriving soon. I sat down on a bench next to the train station. My thoughts began drifting to Rose and I wondered what she was doing and what she was wearing. I caught myself daydreaming. I refocused on the moment and my surroundings.

I observed a young teenage girl with her mother. Our eyes happened to pass each other and then back again. She gave a soft smile and then diverted her attention back to her mom. I kept looking at her for some strange reason until Ismale tapped me on the shoulder. I jumped quickly to my feet. "Are we ready to go?" I asked. "Soon," he replied. "What were you looking at?" "Nothing," I replied. "Keep you wits about you because you never know who is a teacher and who is a student." "What?" I asked. Just at that moment a whistle blasted from the incoming train. The train master yelled "all aboard."

CHAPTER 5
YOU ARE WHAT YOU EAT

We settled into our seats and Ismale announced that he had to go to another compartment to relax. I asked him when he was coming back. "In time," he replied sharply. I began to survey the scene after he left and my eyes caught the same girl from the station. Her seat was facing mine on the other side of the aisle. I smiled quickly and began to busy myself with more important things, like tying my shoes. When I rolled up from my important task I glanced at the girl again and she was staring at me but her mother was gone. She waved at me to come over. I felt a strange comfort to accept her invitation and I took a seat across from her.

"My name is Justine," she said. "I am Q," I said. "Q is an interesting name," she replied. "Does it stand for anything?" "Quirky," I said. "I see that in you," she said. We both smiled, amused by the ease of our conversation.

"Where are you going?" I asked her. "To see my father," she said. "Is that your mother?" I asked. "No, she is my aunt, my father's younger sister Lynn," she said. "Where did she go?" I asked. "She has a friend in the other compartment that she wanted to visit with," she said. We chatted for a while and then she asked me if I knew how to play Crazy Eights. "Crazy Eights, I am the king of Crazy Eights," I proudly replied. "We will see," she said. She pulled out a deck of cards from her purse and began dealing the deck. We just started our fifth game when the steward came around with menus. "I will be back shortly to take your order," he said. "We are tied two games to two," I said. "The next one to win is the grand champion." "You will not be very hungry after this game," she said. "Why?" I asked. "Because you will be eating crow," she stated. The game finished and I was picking feathers out of my bicuspids. The waiter asked us what we would like to eat. Justine ordered the vegetarian burger with a salad. I ordered the chicken dinner, with a beer. "What would you like to drink?" I asked her. "Water is fine," she said.

I began to panic as I realized that I had no money. I excused myself from the table pretending to go to the washroom. I was trying to find Ismale to get some money to pay for our meals. I walked into the next compartment and pulled out my ticket from my pocket and I realized that meals were included. Relieved from the embarrassment of not having any money, I looked up to see Ismale with Justine's aunt. They were talking and laughing. I was going to interrupt them out of curiosity but decided to go back to see Justine. When I arrived back Justine had already put away the cards and was preparing for our meals. "I am starving," I said. "Why are you so hungry?" she asked. "I am always starving," I said. "It is because you eat the wrong foods?" she replied. "What are you talking about?" I asked her. "You eat a lot of meat and dairy, don't you?" "Of course I do, everyone does," I replied. "Not everyone," Justine said.

"Eating meat is stealing from another species that shares this planet with us," Justine said.

"Stealing what?" I asked. "Stealing energy," she replied. "What do you mean?" I asked.

"Imagine for a moment the events that lead up to the slaughtering of an animal," she said. "The cows are all being lined up in this vast line to be killed. As the cows stand in this unknown line, they hear the violent cries of their own species gasp their last breath of life, they smell the thick scent of the draining adrenalin-filled blood in the air and they sense their own fate. A toxic eruption of other brain-induced chemicals flows into their bloodstream as a defense mechanism. The fight-or-flight mechanism we all share on this planet is activated. A chemical cocktail of unknown energy is released into their arteries and pumped violently into their body. Their veins spew out toxic energy from breaking down the last metabolism of nutrients used to combat the fear. The waste products of terror filled their flesh and we as humans eventually consume this meat for our own energy.

"Sound appetizing?" Justine asked. "Not in the least," I replied.

"Where did you learn all that?" I asked. "From my father," she said. "He is an environmental scientist. We are vegetarians for three distinct reasons: ethical, environmental, and health.

"In North America we slaughter over six billion warm-blooded animals a year for meat. The number of animals killed in the U.S. is five hundred thousand per hour. Billions more are exploited each year for egg and dairy products. Dairy cows are kept permanently pregnant. Beef cattle are castrated to ensure docility. Veal comes from calves that are permanently confined to stalls where they cannot turn around or even take a single step. This is done so that their muscles won't develop, making them tender for your dinner plate. Federal regulations allow farm animals to be transported without food or water for thirty-six to seventy-two hours, depending on the species of animal. Approximately three million poultry are destroyed annually in Canada during shipment due to severe heat stress. Overcrowding of animals during shipment cripples seven thousand dairy cows a year that arrive at slaughter plants just in Ontario." "Hold on," I said. "Our government would not allow this to occur." "You wouldn't think so, would you?" she replied.

"In North America, about 85 percent of the grain, corn, and oats grown are to feed cows," she announced with a bit of a temperament. "Around twenty million people in our world die of malnutrition every year. We would rather feed other animals to create meat than feed our own species.

The volume of grain fed to animals so that we could eat meat would feed 1.3 billion people and that is just grain. The land required to support someone on a meat-based diet is four acres, a vegetarian diet one-half acre or less. More than half of all water that we consume is used in livestock production. A pound of wheat requires twenty-five gallons of water; a pound of beef requires five thousand gallons of water. Every eight seconds a tree disappears in North America to create cropland. Damage caused by one one-fourth pound burger equals the loss of one-half ton of plants, animals, and insects. Livestock has four times the population of humans, which produce 2.6 billion tons of waste a year. Unfortunately, we have no proper sewage system to handle all waste and it leaches into the soil and into our waterways. The total excrement by the U.S. population is twelve thousand pounds per second compared to the total excrement by U.S. livestock, which is two hundred fifty thousand pounds per second."

"Unbelievable," I announced. "This information cannot be true. We are too wise of a species to allow this to happen." Justine just looked at me with her eyebrows popped up and her smile in a straight line. "I can't believe all of this," I said. "We are stealing from the animals and our environment to feed the mind's craving for meat," she stated. "Our society is stealing energy and when you steal energy it does not have a positive effect on the health of the person consuming that energy. Examine the health of not only our planet but of a society that predominantly eats meat. Ask yourself why we have so many adverse health effects from consuming another species' flesh. Quietly, ask yourself, why do we suffer heart attacks at the rate of one every twenty-five seconds and strokes every forty-five seconds in just the U.S.? The risk of death from heart attack by an average person is 50 percent. By not eating meat that figure drops to 15 percent.

"Why has cancer become an epidemic in our society? Breast cancer in women is four times higher in women who eat meat daily than women that eat meat less than once a week. The same holds true for men and prostate cancer. Men that eat meat daily have a 3.6 times higher chance of getting cancer than men that eat meat less than once a week."

"Everything you read nowadays causes cancer," I said. "Cancer is a product of man's greed and struggle for power," she said. "We have polluted our water, soil and air for profit. With every action there is an equal and sometimes more violent reaction. That is what has happened to our planet and all species on this earth must pay the price.

"Diabetes and high blood pressure seem to be the norm for most adults. It is all related to the food we eat and our lifestyle. Fast food chains make billions of dollars from consumers that don't understand the value of food and its importance to our health. Everything is super sized and enriched with fat and grease. We triple the burgers and double the amount of French fries we consume. Feedlots are finding it hard to keep up with the demand. They fill animals with hormones and inject them with antibiotics to stop infections. In fact, over

55 percent of livestock are fed antibiotics routinely. Our resistance to penicillin in 1960 was 13 percent but because of the continuing stream of antibiotics pumped into the flesh of animals in 1988 the resistance to penicillin grew to 91 percent. It is all related.

"The connection between everything we do and everything we fail to do, all relates. What someone does in Texas at a feedlot is connected to us. We all share this environment and we are all connected to the same sources of energy. But we have been brainwashed by companies and the government to accept a certain reality based on falsehoods and deceptions.

"The dairy council tells us that we are drinking 2 percent milk but they do not tell us that 2 percent is a figure based on the weight of milk and milk is mostly water; 2 percent is actually 35 percent fat. In fact, the meat and dairy industry advertise openly in every elementary school in almost every community. Their message is constant and consistent: You must consume dairy and meat to be healthy. They were brilliant in their approach. The envy of any business that profited off consumer consumption is what they became. They created the four food groups. They actually created a brainwash procedure that was passed on for generations.

"They were brilliant in their ability to convince humans of what energy sources were best for them and how much that they needed to consume to best survive on this planet. The four food groups were drilled into our mind and reinforced by commercials at home. Drink milk...live life. They should have said drink milk...get fat. Billboards and magazines portray pictures of young, athletic, healthy humans with a milk mustache for profits. We believe all of this because we are programmed to believe and that mindset is most difficult to change and rearrange.

"There is so much information available to people but they choose to ignore and dismiss the information," she concluded. I must have had my mouth open because a drop of saliva poured out of my mouth and onto my plate of food that just arrived. I looked down at the chicken and my stomach began to turn and the smell was making me ill. Justine looked up at me and handed me half of her burger. "I will share this with you if you would like." I shook my head to agree. "This isn't half bad," I said in surprise. "Most products on the market are quite good," she replied. "It is very easy to eat vegetarian today compared to the hippies in the '60s and '70s. More and more people are becoming health conscious and have created a market for a variety of veggie products on the store shelves. I eat chicken nuggets that are really soy nuggets and veggie bacon, ground beef, cutlets, and tofu products."

"Where do you find these products?" I asked. "In the grocery store," she replied impatiently. "They are everywhere you look. You're just not aware of them because you are not looking for them." "You're right," I said. "It is like when you buy a car and suddenly you are driving on the street and you realize that a lot of people drive the same kind of car or when you know someone close to you that is having a baby and suddenly it seems everyone you meet is having a baby," Justine replied. "It is strange how life is when you are aware." Just as we were finishing our meal, Justine's aunt arrived back at the table. I excused myself and went back to see Ismale.

As I sat down, Ismale asked me if I was full from dinner. "Not exactly," I replied. "Why don't you eat meat?" I asked him. "You have had a car to drive haven't you?" he asked. "Yes," I replied. "What kind of gas did you put in the car?" he asked. "What everyone else puts in his or her car," I replied sarcastically. "What if the gas you used was leaded?" he asked. "We don't use leaded gas anymore because we know that it is bad for the environment and unhealthy for our cars," I said. "Exactly," Ismale said with a salient pause. I just looked at him and within a few seconds the light bulb clicked on. Ismale smiled back at me to acknowledge my connection.

"So you're saying that as we evolve and become more aware of things as a society we will slowly eliminate them." "Correct," he said. "The same holds true for fuel in our bodies as it is for our cars. We consume energy to create energy. If the energy you are consuming is from a poor source then you will in turn have poor energy to use and more importantly, exchange. We are what we eat," Ismale stated. "You eat energy that was stolen from another species on this planet, and then you will suffer the by-product of that energy. Heart disease, cancer, diabetes, etc., carry the same fate. Similar to a car, if you put leaded fuel in that car it will over time internally break down the engine in the car.

"The other problems are the emissions that are released. In a car the exhaust will spew out emissions that are harmful to the environment, causing acid rain, global warming, and damage to our soil, water, and air. They are all by-products of using an energy source that wasn't meant to be used by humans. The same holds true for the fuel used to feed our bodies. If the fuel is animal product we will emit energy to resemble that energy. Eating animal products causes many health-related problems in our society. The energy that is consumed to treat those people is amazing. More importantly is the energy those people are trying to share with others. They are sick and frustrated. The energy they share with others is a reflection of how they feel inside. It usually isn't very good energy and it often leads to more energy problems.

"Once we understand that we are a global community and that everything is connected we can help to heal those people. Until then we have serious energy problems in all areas of human existence: environmental, health, social, spiritual, etc. Everything is related and everything counts. That is why I don't eat meat or dairy."

My mouth must have been opened again because I had saliva drops on the front of my shirt. I quickly closed my mouth, swallowed, and gazed out the window. I opened my eyes to the trees that lined the railway tracks and realized that they were all without leaves and they looked tired and sick. The trees farther away all seemed to be healthy and much larger than the trees near the tracks. My eyes felt heavy and they slowly slipped behind my mind.

Screams were coming from the mouth of a mountain. I rushed in to see what the problem was. As I entered I felt a dark and cold breeze on my cheek. Flickering in the distance was a torch attached to the side of this corridor leading further into the mountain. I felt drawn to it like an automobile accident. I had to see what was down there. The corridor was lined with torches burning brightly on each side. By every torch was a large stone door with a wooden handle. I noticed a carving on the first door. It was in the shape of a half moon. The door across had a carving of a star with six points. The next door had a carving of two circles, and next was a triangle, and a door with a sun. There were twelve doors and all of them had a carving. The corridor continued but there were no torches to reveal its path. It darkened quickly and it seemed everlasting. A cold chill entered my body as I stood looking out into the darkness. I walked back and stood amidst all the doors trying to figure out what door I must enter and what doors I must not.

"This must be a test," I thought to myself. I started to panic and began worrying about making a mistake and not passing the test. I was afraid of becoming a failure and not being able to move on in this game, whatever game this was, and my mind was racing in circles. I was becoming dizzy and felt weakened by my fears. Suddenly, I remembered Ismale and his lessons. "Live in the moment" shouted into my mind like an echo in a canyon. I stopped and caught my breath. I began to look carefully at all the carvings and then out of the side of my right eye, I saw a small little creature crawl out of one of the doors and then quickly dart back into the door. I slowly walked over to that door and the carvings revealed four circles all overlapping each other, yet they all seemed to be separate. I thought to myself that a creature is surviving in what is behind this door, so it must be safe. I slowly opened the heavy door to sneak a peek inside. Like a vacuum for humans I was sucked inside the door. My body felt weightless as some strange force carried me into the room. Then I felt gravity at its best. I fell face down onto the dirt floor of the room. My mouth open with anticipation was now filled will dirt and dust. I began to cough in order to clear my throat and began to look up.

It was Ismale. He was shaking my shoulders and asking me if I was all right. I gazed out the window and the flash from the mountains brought me back to reality. "I must have fallen asleep," I said. "You must have had a great dream because you're all wet," he said. I looked down on the table to a pool of saliva that drained from my mouth during my nap. "Where are we?" I asked. "Close to our destination," Ismale responded. "Where are we going?" I asked. "To a friend's place for a while," he responded. I shook my head, confused but reassured that we had a destination.

Ismale excused himself from the table and I sat there alone wondering about my dream. Where was the mountain located? Why all the doors? What happens inside the room? For the first time I started to feel like I had a purpose on this trip. I felt a sense that I was about to embark on this amazing journey. Just as I was feeling worthy of myself, I caught

Justine's aunt staring at me. I looked at her and she smiled. I turned my glance away but she continued to stare. Our eyes met once again and she grinned playfully at me.

I got out of my seat and walked over to her. "Hi," I said. "My name is Q." "I know," she said. "My name is Lynn." "I know," I said in a friendly tone. "Would you join me!" she insisted. I sat down and noticed that Justine was gone. "Where is Justine?" I asked. "She is with Ismale in the next car," she replied.

"You look refreshed," she said. "I had a little nap and I am a little more awake," I said. "Are you truly awake?" she said in a whisper. "What do you mean?" I asked. "Do you really understand our world and your place in it?" she asked. "I think so," I replied. "Justine told me that she talked to you about the connection we share with the planet and with what we eat." "Yes, she blew me away with all the facts and information that she knew for a teenager." "A special man has taught her, my brother," she proclaimed. "What is your brother's name?" I asked. "Lorax," she replied. "Lorax," I bounced back to her like an Indian rubber ball. "Yes, my brother is Lorax," she said. "Who is Lorax?" I asked anxiously. "He is my brother," she replied sarcastically. "Seriously, what does he do?" I asked. "He is a man that has been chosen to protect our environment and help save our earth. He is a healer, a philosopher, a guide, and most importantly a teacher. His destiny is to help man understand the rings of truth about our environment," she said.

"I don't understand," I said. "Why are government officials searching for him? Why is Ismale searching for him? Why are people in general searching for him?" I asked. "He speaks the truth and the truth is not always profitable to corporations, lobby groups, and policy makers, such as politicians. My brother has made enemies out of some very powerful people because he is trying to inform people of the corruption and deception. We must protect him and continue the work that he has started," she said. "I still don't understand," I stated.

"I will try and explain but Ismale and Scott will provide you with more information later tonight," she said. "Who is Scott?" I interrupted. "He is a healer," she announced quickly. "It all revolves around energy. If society used renewable sources of energy they would be constant and remain for generations. The reality is that they have little long-term financial benefits to the corporations that supply energy. The massive oil cartels and the giant hydro and gas companies would suffer greatly. Suffer in dollar amounts and those lost dollars would affect the contributions to politicians.

"Unfortunately, we allow lobby groups to finance political futures and aspirations. This process of investing time and energy into the future roles of potential and current politicians has been the greatest barrier to our advancements as a species. Lobby groups are investing in politicians that will allow big business to advance and profit regardless of the effect it will have on our planet and the species that share it. The energy of power and greed is overwhelming to those individuals that crave it. There is a symbiotic relationship that is shared between profit and the advancement of political goals.

"Ultimately, the victim is the environment and all the species that feed from the environment. Travel back thirty years and tell a resident of that era that in three decades the purchasing of bottled water would be a billion-dollar industry. Now, fast-forward thirty years and ask a person on the streets where they get their drinking water from. It would be interesting to hear the answer that they would share.

"We have only been on this planet a relatively short duration and decades will dissolve into minutes on the chart of environmental disasters man has created. Analyze the recent changes in our environment and compare these findings to the last one hundred years. We have polluted more of our environment in the last thirty years than in the total history of our evolution. This pattern is exponentially climbing with no end in sight, except total destruction."

"Where have you learned all of this?" I asked. "I am an environmental science teacher," she replied. "I have spent the last twenty years of my life researching and teaching students about the problems in our environment. Tropical rain forest destruction, acid rain, ozone depletion, soil erosion, water contamination, Great Lakes pollution, and of course global warming."

"You are an alarmist, you worry too much about the future," I replied. "Take a moment and consider the life of our future generations if what I am saying is right," she said. "The three elements critical to our survival are all being destroyed equally: air, soil, and water. Fortunately, we have the blueprint and ability to save this planet. It all revolves around the consumption and use of energy. That is what Lorax is doing. He is laying out the drawings and informing the public on what to do." "If this is good for our planet, then why are people after him?" I asked. "Lorax is designing and advocating many innovative and high-tech ideas. Ideas that will cause huge financial losses to big business." Quietly I felt a hand rest upon my shoulder; it was Ismale. "We must prepare to go," Ismale said. I thanked Lynn for her time and wished her well on her journey.

Ismale and I returned to our seats. "Did you have a pleasant talk?" Ismale inquired. "I did," I said. "But who is Scott?" I asked. "Scott is a friend of mine that will be helping us out in our journey." "What does Scott do?" I asked. "He is a master on healing touch," Ismale replied. "He teaches and has a private practice." "Where does he live?" I asked. "He lives in a small village outside of Winnipeg," Ismale said. The train conductor announced our stop. "Are we in Winnipeg?" I asked. "Yes, we are at the halfway point of our journey and like many things in life the second half is the most difficult," Ismale said with a sharp tongue.

I quietly thought to myself my journey thus far. I climbed into a truck and learned about living in the moment. I entered a diner and learned about sharing and stealing energy. I stepped into a library and learned about agreeing with your self. And I just hopped on to a train and learned that we are what we eat. Is there a connection to all of these doorways? Am I being guided by something or somebody other than myself? What is going to happen to me next? Where is Rose, when I need her?

Stop, quiet the mind and quit worrying; I have Ismale to blame for anything that goes wrong.

CHAPTER 6
DREAM CATCHER

We stepped off the train. I noticed a woman back beyond the tracks in a long jacket. The hood of her jacket hid her face. She looked familiar but I could barely see her through the traffic. Ahead, I saw Ismale embrace this rather tall and muscular man. They hugged for a long time and then they released and hugged again. I walked toward them, still looking at the woman to get a glimpse at her face but she turned and walked away. I sensed that it was Rose but reality was imposing its will saying that it couldn't be. Ismale introduced me to Scott. I put out my hand to say hi but he grabbed me and gave me a huge bear hug. "It is a pleasure to meet you Q," he said. "I have heard many wonderful things about you and I look forward to us sharing some tea and conversations."

Scott was not what I thought a healer would look like. He kind of looked like Tom Selleck, strong and masculine but kind and gentle. For some reason, I was thinking of someone like Gandhi or Richard Simmons. I wasn't sure but he wasn't what I had envisioned. We walked to Scott's jeep and loaded our bags. I noticed someone sitting in the front passenger's seat. I moved around the Jeep to get a better look and realized that it was the woman in the station. The door opened and the woman jumped out and grabbed me, her hood still up. I didn't know who it was until she whispered in my ear, "I missed you." "Rose!" I yelled out. I pushed her hood down to reveal her face and without a thought I gave her a kiss. She kissed back and I hugged her again. Ismale interrupted and told us to get a room. "Get in the Jeep. We have a long ride ahead," Ismale proclaimed. Rose and I sat in the back seat while Scott and Ismale sat in the front. The ride took about two hours to Scott's place, which gave me and Rose plenty of time to catch up. I was excited to tell her about my stories and all the people I met. We talked until our tongues tired and our stories grew familiar. When we arrived at Scott's house it was late and very dark. He lived in a log house deep in the woods far away from civilization. The house was large like a chalet. A huge fireplace built in rocks filled the room with the aroma of burning wood and the great outdoors. We were all given a room to sleep in; I was hoping to share a room with Rose but it wasn't meant to be. A hot meal greeted us and so did Scott's friend Marianne. We all sat down to feast on a vegetarian stew that was outstanding. The trip and the meal made it a short night. As I drifted into my silent sleep, my mind rehearsed the day's events and I realized that I had stepped into doorways three and four. The library and the train—*knowledge and tracks of time*, I thought to myself, as I slipped into the dark night.

The next morning we were awakened by the sound of a gun blasting outside the cabin. I peered out the bedroom window and saw Scott holding a shotgun in his arms with a large black bear racing away in the freshly fallen snow. It was like a scene out of Hollywood, yet it was so surreal. I quickly dressed and flew downstairs to find out what was going on. Scott and Ismale were just walking through the door laughing. They both seemed to be in a state of euphoria and exhilaration. "Good morning," Scott announced with joy and freshness in his voice. "How did you sleep?" he asked. "Like a child," I responded. "Welcome to the great outdoors," Ismale proclaimed. "What are we having for breakfast?" I asked. "Black bear soup," Ismale said with a smile.

We all sat down at a large wooden table to have a cup of tea and some toast. "What is on the agenda today?" I asked. "A little adventure," Scott replied. "We are going for a hike up the mountain to find something," he said. "What are we looking for?" I asked. "We are going hunting for sanctuary," Scott said. Just as I was about to ask him what he meant, Marianne walked into the cabin. "We are all set," she announced. Rose walked into the room and walked up to me and whispered into my ear. "Fight the good fight," she said. She then grabbed my hand and I had a vision of an eagle high in its flight climbing to the top of a snow-covered mountain. It landed on a cliff on the side of this large mountain. From a bird's-eye view, I could see a beautiful black bear and its cubs playing in the snow. She released my hand and I sank into my seat. "Where are we going?" I shrieked. "Not to worry my good man," Ismale said. "We are going on a little journey to a sacred place high into the mountains for a little steam." I was about to inquire more about our trip but decided to stay silent and go with the flow.

We all were dressed like Eskimos, or so I thought. "It must be very cold where we are going," I stated. "The layers you wear are only temporary," Scott stated. "We as humans dress for each occasion but it is what is on the inside that counts," he said. As I stepped out of the cabin and onto the porch, I was greeted by the bright smile of the sun. The snow glistened with the rays of the morning. Our journey began with Scott handing me a branch. "Don't let this branch change in any shape or form. It is needed to fulfill our journey and you must pay close attention to its identity," he said. "What are you talking about?" I asked. Rose grasped my hand. "Keep it whole and don't let it get damaged by our climb," she said. "Okay," I said. Not knowing its significance or meaning, I looked at Scott and sarcastically told him, "I will be the protector of this branch and commit my life to keeping it alive."

We traveled for most of the morning on a steady climb up the mountain's face. Several times I lost my footing and sacrificed my balance in order to keep the branch from breaking. Rose and I were far enough from the others that I could talk to her without feeling they could listen. "How do you know Ismale?" I asked quietly. "Ismale has been a friend of my family for a long time and he is like an uncle to me. He has worked with my father for many years and it seems like I have known him all my life," she said. "Why is he so protective of you?" I asked. "Have you ever wondered if you were born in the wrong family?" she said. "Well, Ismale must ask that question every day because he never knew his real parents. He was placed in an orphanage when he was a baby and he was adopted by parents that couldn't have their own child. He was greatly loved until his thirteenth birthday. On his thirteenth birthday his adopted mother gave birth to a child of her own. Imagine having a brother born on your same birthday. From that moment on, Ismale was always second best and never worthy of their love anymore. Much of what happened throughout his life cannot be blamed on Ismale.

"However, his own actions showed that he had chosen to be part of the problem and not part of the solution. He began getting into trouble at school and eventually he dropped out. He was on his own and on streets by the time he was sixteen years old. He struggled for many years until he happened to meet Lorax. Lorax gave him a job and he became his first protégé. Ismale has many wonderful and difficult experiences in life to share and teach from. Did you know that he was once married? She died a few years ago from cancer. He loved her with all of his heart, mind, and soul. Ismale is a great man with many insights into life. He is a wonderful teacher and I was one of his best students, at least that is what he tells me." Rose looked up to the others and they were almost at the top of the mountain. "Just trust Ismale and keep your mind and heart open to his words but now is time for you to listen to your own words. We are here," she announced.

Near the top of the mountain was a clearing. As we grew closer I saw what I thought was a tepee or wigwam. I asked Scott if he ever heard the joke about the man that went to a psychologist because he was having trouble sleeping. He said he hadn't. I continued, "A man walks into a psychologist's office and said, 'doc, I keep having these strange dreams at night. One night I dreamed that I was a tepee and the next night I dreamed I was a wigwam.'

"The doctor looked at him confidently and said, 'your problem is simple, you are two tents.' Get it? Too tense." He chuckled to amuse me but he was distracted with the destination. As we came closer to the tepee I asked, "What is a tepee doing way up here?" "It is a sweat hut," Scott replied. "A sweat hut for what?" I asked. "To cleanse your body and awaken your spirit," he replied. "Speak softly; there are many ears up here."

The landing where the sweat hut was located was surrounded by many large rocks and carefully placed evergreen leaves. They created a path to a fire pit that was filled with burning red-hot rocks. Surrounding the hut were more evergreen leaves that were laid out precisely in a circle with a pathway to enter the hut. We sat around the fire pit to get warm and rehydrate.

Scott looked at me with a serious tone in his eyes. He told me to listen attentively. "The logs are the old men; they are sacred and wise. They have grown for generations and have been witness to many seasons of life. They provide us with warmth and shelter. The large rocks are the grandfathers. They provide shape and texture to our world. They were conceived with this planet and have endured since the beginning of time. They have been polished and cut by the passing of time. They have seen all and stand silently. They have listened to every sound and speak only when fully appreciated. The grandfathers give unconditionally. They represent the wisest and have the most understanding of our culture. They know where we have been and where we are going. Today they may speak to you and help you understand yourself more fully. They may provide visions of your journey. You must open your heart and clear your mind to fully accept their stories."

I felt a rush of adrenalin dump into my body. I was excited and scared at the same time. It felt like going on a monster rollercoaster's slowing uphill climb. "You must follow my orders exactly, do you understand?" Scott said. "Yes," I replied. "Give me the branch," he ordered. I handed the branch. He stared at it for a moment and then he looked at me. "You have taken good care of this branch and you are worthy of its friendship. Take the branch and place it in the fire," Scott said. I placed the branch on top of one of the large burning red rocks. It slowly began to crackle and spark. "It is thanking you for helping it on its journey," Scott said. Then he threw some dry evergreen leaves on the fire and it erupted with flames. "It is time," Scott said. "You must not disturb the leaves on the ground," he stated. "Take off your jacket, snow pants, and boots," he said.

The hut was covered with thick blankets and Marianne revealed a small opening. I was following Ismale as I entered the hut and Rose followed Marianne. In the middle of the hut was a large hole in the ground. "You must enter clockwise," Ismale said. Crawling on our hands and knees we moved around the hole. Scott then slipped in a bucket of water and some spices. He then brought four of the scalding hot rocks from the fire pit outside of the hut. As each rock was placed in the hole, Ismale stroked it with a large feather. "Welcome grandfather," Ismale said to each rock. The hut was getting rather hot but comfortable. When I was young my father would take me to a steam bath in his old neighborhood. I always remembered going on a Saturday and spending most of the afternoon taking a hot steam and then resting on rows of beds. Many men would bring food from home and vodka. They would eat and drink in between steams. It was a fond memory because the energy was good, I thought to myself.

Scott entered the hut and sealed the door. Not a visible light could be seen, except the red heat falling off the rocks. Scott placed some spices on the rocks and said that it would help with our breathing by opening up our lungs. It did, until he splashed water on the rocks. The steam filled my nostrils like burning lava. It crashed into my head and caught my breath. I slowly settled into a comfortable breath when he splashed more water on the rocks and then he began a chant. Ismale and Marianne joined him as I panicked to catch my breath.

They finished their chant with another splash of water on the rocks. I wanted to leave and ask Scott to stop splashing water on the rock but I didn't. I began to focus on my breathing and slowly I began to relax. Scott interrupted the silence by stating that he wanted to tell a story. "There was once a man who was a stonecutter. Unhappy with his role in life, he questioned God why he had to be a stonecutter. He asked God if he could be someone more successful and admired. He asked if he could be a king. God asked him why he wanted to be a king. A king is someone that is rich and important. Someone that people look up to, he replied. A king you want to be, a king you will be. The man was now the king. The years, they passed and the man became bored and discouraged with his responsibilities as a king so he asked God if he could be a bird. God replied, why do you want to be a bird? A bird is free and flies without worries. It doesn't have to care for people and make important decisions every day. A bird you want to be, a bird you will be. The man was now a bird, flying freely over the kingdom and enjoying the skies until the wind picked up and tossed the bird about. The man didn't like being controlled by the wind and asked God if he could become the wind. God asked, why do you want to be the wind? The wind is great and powerful. It controls the birds in flight and moves the skies. The wind you want to be, the wind you will be. The man was now the wind. The wind moved the clouds and played with the birds but it could not move the mountain. I would like to be the mountain, the man thought. He asked God if he could be the mountain. God asked, why do you want to be the mountain? The mountain is not moved by the wind, it is strong and majestic. It stands tall and powerful. The mountain you want to be, the mountain you will be. The man became the mountain. The man then began to feel himself change and the mountain was being carved by something. God, the mountain is so large and powerful, how can anything change the mountain? God paused and then told him that you are right, the mountain is strong. It is powerful and true, but a stonecutter has the tools to change its shape and the strength to carve it."

Scott then opened the door and we all exited going clockwise around the rocks. Carefully we traveled the path leading toward the fire pit for some water. I was totally drenched from sweat and so were the others. "Rose, you look like a wet puppy," I said. She just smiled and looked away. I sensed something was wrong with Rose. She said little during breakfast and less on our journey up the mountain. "Are you okay?" I asked her. "I am fine," she replied. "I just have to rest and quiet my mind. I will be okay." Scott announced that the next time we go into the hut that it would just be him and I. "Go in again? Are you crazy?" I said. "I thought we were done." "Not exactly," Scott replied. "We actually do this three times but today we are only going to do it twice." "Why just you and me?" I inquired. "It is time for you to get connected," Scott replied. "Connected with what?" I said. Scott just smiled and pointed me toward the hut. I entered exactly the same way as the first time. Scott followed and then Ismale placed three more fire-drenched rocks into the pit. Each time, Scott greeted the grandfathers and stroked them as they were placed in the pit. The fourth rock was quite large and it broke into several pieces as Ismale placed it in the pit. "That is a good sign," Scott said.

He sealed the hut and placed water and more spices on the rocks. He added a splash of water and asked me to concentrate on my journey thus far. I began thinking about how I had met Ismale and Rose and the doors that I have entered, but my mind kept racing to my dream on the train and brought me back to the doors in the mountain. Scott interrupted me by telling me not to fight where my mind wanted to go. He told me that a spirit will guide me to my thoughts and to fight the spirit is like fighting a ghost. He told me to breathe deeply and relax my body. My mind began to settle into the vision of the dream I had on the train.

I remembered opening the door with the four circles that were attached and falling to the ground face first. I opened my eyes and I saw a narrow room filled with candles leading down a hallway. I walked down the hallway to find another large wooden door. This door had no markings on it except a gold handle in the shape of a dragon. As I moved to place my hand on it, fire puffed out of its mouth. I tried again and another puff of fire exploded from its mouth. I stood there wondering how I could open this door. Perhaps I should go back, I thought. Go back to what? A dragon breathing fire to prevent the door from being opened! How could I stop the dragon from breathing fire? I have no water and no extinguisher. I was born the year of the dragon, I thought. The fire is fear. Fear not what is behind the door and you may enter. "Who said that?" I thought. Was that me or is someone in my head? I closed my eyes to eased my mind and thought of God, strangely enough. I reached for the handle and opened the door.

I was on top of a mountain looking down on a war of men. They were fighting with swords and knives, dressed in armor from the kings they honored. There were four distinct sets of armor fighting and protecting four different sides. They were dressed in distinct colors of armor. The ones to the north were dressed in white, the east in green, the south in yellow, and the west in blue. They were not fighting each other. They were fighting outward in a box shape and protecting the middle. They were fighting men dressed in gold and silver cloaks with hoods drawn over their faces. The men dressed in gold and silver came in waves and were slowly penetrating into the box. In the middle of the box was a man sitting on the ground. The men fought fiercely to protect this man. Thousands of men were dying and the battle was massive. The gold and silver men were breaking through the box on the west side and then the man in the middle stood up. His head was still drawn toward the ground; he slowly raised his head and quietly turned toward me. Oblivious to the conflict that surrounded him and his ultimate doom, he raised his right arm and pointed toward me. His forefinger stretched out and in that moment a sword from a gold warrior pierced his back and came out of his chest. The man stood silent, then a lightning bolt erupted from his finger and struck me. I fell back behind the door and onto the ground.

Light entered the hut as Scott opened the door. "Time to go," he said. Confused, I said nothing and left the hut. Still in a state of shock I sat on a log outside of the hut by the fire pit. Silently, I looked out into the distance. "Are you okay?" Rose asked. "I am not sure," I replied. Ismale looked at me and asked me to share my vision. I described every detail in my vision without interruption. When I finished, I felt weak and angry. "Who is the man that was killed? Why did he have to die? Who were the men in armor? Who were the men in gold and silver? What was the man in the middle trying to pass on to me?" I asked Ismale.

"These are your questions to be answered," Ismale stated. "You must find the answers in your journey." "That's not fair," I responded angrily. "I did not ask for this journey, I did not want to take this trip." "But you are here now," Ismale said. "What do you want to do with you time you have?" he asked in a somber tone.

"I have no idea," I replied defensively. "Think," Ismale said. "Think about what?" I asked. "About your vision," he responded. "I will but not now," I said.

Scott interrupted and announced that we must make our way back before it got too dark. We packed up our things and left. The walk down seemed more difficult than the hike up the mountain. My mind was filled with many thoughts but not one would remain long enough for me to enjoy. We made our way back to the cabin and I went straight to my bedroom to rest. I lay quietly with my thoughts and soon fell fast asleep. I awoke to voices talking in the living room; I threw on a new face and joined the group. "How are you feeling?" Scott inquired. "I am fine," I said. "So what is going on?" I asked. "We are just having a little chat about life and how man screwed it all up," Ismale said. "There is hot soup on the stove when you are hungry," Marianne said. "Thanks, I am hungry now," I replied. "Where is Rose?" I asked. "She went for a walk," Marianne said.

"Soup smells great", I announced. "Hope you enjoy it," Ismale said, "but stop interrupting us." "The advancement of humans has unlimited boundaries," Ismale continued. "Just study our relatively short stay on this planet. We quickly learned how to take our only source of energy and convert it to maintain our survival and our continued evolution. The problem that exists is our interpretation of how to use this life-dependant energy source. History reveals an immediate stealing of energy. If your faith is creation, the Bible shares the story of Adam and Eve. The first act that we are told in this story is that Eve stole an apple from the Garden of Eden and had Adam eat the apple. The seeds of that apple have been planted in every human since that time."

"Why has God allowed us to make all of these mistakes?" I asked. "Because he loves you," Scott replied. "He loves the destruction of this earth that he gave us," I responded in anger. "He loves to see us torture and kill other men and women," I continued. "He loved us so much that he gave us his greatest gift," Scott said. "What is that?" I demanded. "The freedom of choice," he said. "Choice is a special gift and God's love is unconditional," Ismale replied. "If we were without choice and freedom we would not be able to experience all of our senses and all of our fates." "A God that allows for murder, raping, stealing and corruption is not a fair God at all," I said.

"There is a story about Daniel and his king," Scott announced. "Daniel was a high advisor to the king. He shared this duty with two other men. The king favored Daniel over the other two advisors and this angered them. So they devised a plan to remove Daniel from the king's court. They knew that Daniel would never compromise his loyalty and love to God. Therefore, the other two advisors convinced the king that for thirty days the citizens and the court would only pray to the king and anyone that didn't would be thrown in a lion's den."

"I have heard this story before," I interrupted. "You have?" Scott inquired. "Yes, Daniel was thrown into the lion's den but was never eaten because God sent down angels to close the lion's mouth," I said. "What is the moral of the story, Q?" Scott asked. I thought for a moment. "Stay true to your God and you will be saved," I said. "You are right," Scott said, "but what else?" "What do you mean, 'what else?'" I replied. "What else is being told in the story?" Scott asked. "I don't know," I responded defensively. "God gave us the ability to choose and the freedom to make choices," Scott said. "He didn't force a law like the other two advisors did. He allows us to make whatever choices we want and if our convictions are strong and true, he will save us. It is difficult to allow someone you love the freedom to make a choice you know is an obvious mistake and still love them.

"A parent must do this all the time. They make rules and punish if the rules are not followed. If a child continues to break the rules, some parents will then discontinue their love to the child as punishment. They will sever their hearts and abandon their own bloodline because they disagree with choices; choices that God gave us as his gift. Ironically, most children are just repeating the behavior of their parents and they are being punished because of the guilt a parent feels when they witness their child's sins. God allows us to make mistakes and wrong choices but he never stops loving us. He is our greatest parent and we must model ourselves after his parenting skills. He gave the life of his son to us. What greater sacrifice can a parent make?"

"I understand that we have the ability to make choices and that we all make poor choices, but why doesn't God create an environment where all good will occur and bad will not?" I asked. "Free will," Ismale cheerfully announced. "God gave us the freedom to make choices and the freedom to lead a life that we choose. God doesn't interrupt free will and neither can you. God will plant seeds but it is up to you to cultivate them. God has given you all the answers, yet we as a society still choose to ignore them," he said. "Where is the answer?" I asked. "Where do you think?" Ismale said sarcastically. I thought for a minute and said, "In the Bible." "Bingo," Ismale said. "All the writings in the Bible give us the blueprint to our purpose on this planet and beyond. But the only person that has control over his or her destiny is himself or herself. The only person you can control is you and only you. Always understand that you cannot control anyone else or the decisions they make. They have their own free will and that is their God-given right. We choose because we are allowed to make choices. Good choice or bad, they are ours to make. Once a person understands this concept they can move to a deeper understanding of God's will in our lives." "I choose to have more soup," I said with a loud grin.

I moved over to the stove to pour some more soup and as I did Rose walked in with sadness in her eyes. I sensed that she was upset and asked her if she was okay. "I am fine," she said. Ismale noticed her melancholy and asked her to take a seat next to him. "Your heart is troubled," Ismale whispered. "I have seen an awful vision," Rose proclaimed. "Will you share it with us?" Ismale asked. Rose turned her eyes toward me and slowly turned away. "I had a vision about Lorax," she proclaimed. "Many violent people are looking for him and I fear for his life. I have seen Lorax near the top of a mountain on a landing. He is next to a small fire and is sitting with another man. The sun has fallen from the horizon and the glow from the falling rays reveals many shadows moving towards him. They are close to where he is and I am afraid that they will find him soon."

Ismale held Rose in a warm embrace and asked all of us to pack our things because we were to leave immediately. He asked Scott to search the Internet for the earliest flight to Victoria, British Columbia. For the first time I realized the magnitude of our journey. A man I never met before is being hunted down because he had the courage to reveal the truth. "We must protect him," I blurted out. "We must ensure his safety at any cost." Ismale looked at me. "Is that your choice? Because you may be harmed," he said. "I fear the future no longer," I said. "So be it," Ismale responded. "Good," I said. "You have no control over what is about to happen anyway," Ismale replied. Scott came back into the room and told us that the next flight available was at 7:40 a.m. "We must try and get some sleep before we depart," Ismale said. "We will need all our strength for the road ahead." Each of us departed to our separate rooms.

Scott stopped me at my bedroom door and handed me a small black book. It had a hard cover and was filled with lined paper. "You need to take notes and write down your thoughts," he said. "The mind forgets quickly all the little moments that define one's life," he continued. I sat at a desk in my room and opened the book to reveal the first page. The crisp binding crackled as I washed my hand across its crease. I looked for a pen and couldn't find one. I remembered the pen that Charley had given me at the restaurant. I pulled it out and it had an inscription on it. I rolled it around my fingertips to reveal what it said... "Sharing is God's gift." "Sharing what?" I said to myself. I was trying to think of a title for my notes and like a paper cut it hit me without me noticing. I wrote on the top of the first page "**Looking For Lorax**." I placed the pen and book into my bag and turned off the light and within a moment I fell asleep.

CHAPTER 7
WEB OF LIFE

I was abruptly awakened by the cold darkened night. Ismale was pulling on my blankets. "It's time to go, pack quickly," he said. He handed me a brown paper bag and told me to put it away with my things. "Don't open it unless we separate," he said. I put the bag inside one of my sweaters and gathered all my belongings. When I arrived downstairs everyone was packed and ready to go. "No breakfast," I proclaimed. Ismale threw me a blueberry bagel. "Let's roll," he said. The ride was somber, like the crisp cold night air. "What time is it?" I asked. "4 a.m.," Scott replied. I looked at Rose and asked her if she was okay. She smiled and placed her head on my shoulder. The drive was quiet but refreshing. We arrived at the airport in silence.

Scott dropped us off at the departure terminal and he gave us all a warm hug goodbye. He gave me one of his traditional bear hugs and placed a necklace around my neck. I asked him what it was. "It is to ward off evil spirits," he said with a quiet laugh. He tucked the medallion into my sweater before I had a chance to see it. I thanked him for his hospitality as we departed into the terminal. Ismale left to get the tickets as Rose and I sat in a coffee shop. I looked at Rose. "Smile," I said. She tried to present her teeth but could only manage to lift her lips enough to cross her face. "What is wrong?" I asked. "My heart is heavy with sorrow. I fear for my uncle's life," she replied. "What uncle?" I asked. "My father's brother, Lorax," she answered softly. "Lorax is your uncle," I said with astonishment. "He is and his life is in danger. I can feel it in my heart," she said.

"You told me that you didn't know Lorax," I replied harshly. "I wasn't sure that I could trust you," Rose replied softly. "What else do I not know about you?" I responded in bewilderment. "My middle name is Anne," she said. "Well, my middle name is Richard," I replied. "You have a middle name?" Rose asked. "Yes, Q Richard is my name," I said. "Fear not the future it is unknown," I said, remembering the line from the motel. Rose sat up in her seat and presented a wide grin. "Thanks, that is my uncle's saying," she responded with enthusiasm. "I know," I said. "That is why I said it." "You are right, there is nothing I can do about it and the most important thing is taking care of this moment," she replied.

Ismale arrived with the tickets in hand. He announced that we must get going. The plane ride was uneventful because I had to sit by myself. However, I did get a chance to look at the medallion. It had two circles overlapping one another. It was strange as I studied the circles because there was exactly the same amount of space inside the circles as outside. A symbolism of life, I thought. The connection we share with others. Two complete circles that share as much as they don't share. We must always have part of who we are unattached, I thought. It reminded me of the four circles on the door in my dream. They were all connected by the exact same amount, inside and outside. Why four on the door, and why four sides to protect the man in the middle? Why the different colors and who was that man in the middle? My thoughts were interrupted by the announcement of our arrival. Ismale and Rose were ahead of me as we departed the plane. I noticed at the gate a couple of airport workers and two RCMP officers. They were checking all the passengers' IDs and their carry-on bags. As we stood in line, Ismale looked back at me and told me not to forget about the brown bag. He seemed nervous and anxious as he presented his ID to the officers. The officer showed Ismale's ID to one of the RCMP officers. They walked over to Ismale and asked him if he would go with them. Rose was next in line. "Don't say a word," she whispered to me. Her ID was taken and so was she. When I presented my ID one of the workers asked me if I was with them. I felt like Peter and said "no." Confused, I sat on a seat in the terminal to clear my mind. I wondered to myself, why was I sitting alone on the plane and why was my ticket purchased on Scott's Visa and not Ismale's? Ismale must have known that there was a chance of him being detained. Once again, I was alone without friends, money, or a place to go.

I reached inside my bag and pulled out the brown paper bag that Ismale gave me. Inside I found two hundred dollars, a small paper note and a gold key with the inscription "*Lorax.*" I noticed that the old copper ring wasn't in the bag. I unfolded the note and it read, "Godfree - 1234 Lerkim Drive." Godfree. What a cool name, I thought to myself. I need to make a plan, I thought. I must find out where they took Rose and Ismale and what they are going to do with them. I stuffed my jacket into my bag and walked up to one of the security guards at the gate. I told him that the woman in front of me had my jacket. I told him that she asked me on the plane if she could wear it because she was cold. I told him that the RCMP officers took her away and that the address to my cousin's house was in the coat pocket. He told me to wait a minute. When he returned he told me to follow him. We entered a door that led to many small conference rooms inside the airport. I saw Ismale in one of the rooms and across the hall was Rose. The guard told me to stay where I was and that he would be right back. Rose saw me and slowly lifted her index finger to her lips, telling me to be quiet. As I moved closer to Rose she whispered to me that Ismale and she were going to be charged with obstruction of the law if they didn't tell them where Lorax was. "What do you want me to do?" I asked her. "Don't let them know that you are with us," she said. "Ismale gave you a name of a friend, you must find him. He will help you find Lorax and you must give him the key," she said. I was about to ask her what the key was for, when the guard came back with one of the RCMP officers. "Do you know this woman?" he asked. No, I thought this was the lady that had my jacket but I was wrong," I replied. "Get him out of here," the officer instructed the guard. The guard escorted me back into the terminal. "Sorry about the jacket," he said. "Thanks for trying," I replied.

I got into a taxi and instructed the driver to take me to 1234 Lerkim Drive. Thirty-seven dollars later, I arrived at the house. I knocked on the door and a man with gray hair and a slim build answered the door. "I am looking for Godfree," I announced. "Who are you?" the man asked. "I am a friend of Ismale and Rose," I replied. "I have been expecting you," he said with excitement. "Where are Ismale and Rose?" he asked. "They were arrested by RCMP officers at the airport." Godfree's smile sank into his face. "Are they okay?" he asked. "I don't know for sure but they told me that I must find you," I said. "Come in," he said. "I am sorry to burden you with this but I don't know what to do next. I am without a compass or a guide, I don't know where to go next," I stated. "You have a heart and all your sense?" Godfree asked. "Yes, but—" I began to answer. "Yes, but nothing," he replied. "It is all within you," he said.

Godfree walked toward his kitchen. "Are you hungry?" he asked. "I have prepared some vegetable lasagna and garlic bread," he said. "Starving," I replied.

We sat down to eat and I asked him how he knew Ismale and Rose. "I met them through my good friend Lorax," he replied. "I am a retired professor of literature and philosophy at the University of Lethbridge. I taught for twenty-two years and I met Lorax during one of my conferences. I never met a more intriguing person in my life. I was instantly captivated by his personality and his wit. Lorax and I have become very good friends over the years." "What do you do?" I asked. "I write a grassroots paper on the troubles of our society. It was Lorax that encouraged me to start writing again," he said. "Where is Lorax?" I asked impatiently. "I'm not totally sure where he is," Godfree replied. I caught a glimpse at a plaque that was hanging on the wall and the name on it was "Godfree." "Is that how you spell your name?" I asked as I pointed at the plaque. "Yes it is," he replied. "Does your name mean without God?" I asked. "No, on the contrary, I am free because of God," Godfree said. "My mother Iona was a God-fearing woman and she gave me that name because she always knew that I would be set free in life if I allowed God to control it. When we as humans finally realize that we are not in control of our lives and allow God to take control then we become free. "Free from what?" I asked. "Free from guilt, shame, fear, and all other human problems that we claim in our lives. In your journey you must understand that God is guiding you if you are aware. If you give your free will to God and allow God to take control of the wheel then you can enjoy the ride. I am free because I allow God to drive my life.

"Help me clear the table and then we will sit down for a little chat," he added. He walked me to a room at the back of his house. Beautiful glass doors opened to a sunroom with a telescope in the corner and two brown couches. "Sit down," he said sharply. "Speak nothing until I am finished," he said. This room has two doors in it. The one you just entered through and the one that leads outside. At the end of this discussion you must decide what door you are going to use. It will be your choice and your choice only. I will not judge or challenge your decision. Do you understand?" he asked. I nodded with a heavy heart.

"Listen closely to what I am about to tell you," he said. "Don't listen with just your ears but try and listen with your heart," he said, staring right through me. Once again I nodded slowly. "The human condition is made up of so many emotions. To capture and firmly understand these infinite emotions is the gift God granted to humans. To understand and accept all of our senses is an essential part of the journey. Failing to understand our emotions is like living without a limb. It is the feeling of being crippled or paralyzed. The emotions that we embrace in our daily life define the silhouette of our being. The shadow is narrow with simple understanding and wider with a fuller understanding. The blessed emotions that we have been given carry an unyielding burden when misunderstood.

"Fear, sorrow, guilt, regret, and remorse are emotions that have been passed down from generation to generation. They have become a breeding ground of bacteria placed in a dish that has been accidentally pushed over the edge of our learning desks. They have been cultivated in a classroom filled with ignorance and deception. They have been placed in our fertile minds by the serpent, spreading without warning, and contaminating every living being in its path.

"I will try and illustrate what I mean. I was in paradise, filled with lush trees and green grass. A rainbow of colors raced across the land from the flowers. There was a babbling brook running through the middle of the land, separating two massive trees. One tree was older. It was full of fruit and stood majestic overlooking the land. The other tree was younger and overflowing with juicy fruit. The young tree was forbidden to be eaten from because it was not fully developed. It was not ready for the lips of man. Yet, a man and a woman were captivated by the abundance of the tree's fruit. They were drawn to the tree by an evil tongue. They ate all the fruit from the forbidden tree. Seeds of the fruit were falling from their mouths and contaminating the soil all around.

"Contagious was the spread of these seeds. By the fruit we know the tree. It has taken root in the fertile grounds of our minds' belief system. The tree reveals who we are and what truths we believe. The tree was evil and the tree is contaminated with the poison of lies. The lies of our emotions that tell us that we are not good enough to live as God intended. The lies that created fear and doubt, regret and remorse, hate and guilt. The lies have been nourished and strengthened by man. They have been communicated and passed on by each society man has created. Hope is near. Hope is found in the collective unconsciousness of man. A more enriched understanding of who we are and what we are meant to do. The more we question the prince of lies the weaker he becomes. The more we communicate unconscious thoughts the more powerful our immune system becomes. The more we question the less the lies grow. The more questions the weaker the virus grows. The more we communicate consciously and through the unconscious the more powerful our immune system is to resist the prince of lies.

Failure is not an option. If we fail it will be like a warm summer tornado that passes through and leaves lost homes and destroyed lives in its aftermath. We cannot afford to fail in our strife to bring forth a better quality of life for our next generation. A generation that needs to be taught that greed, power, and money is not more important than compassion, love, and mutual respect. The next generation must be taught by the greatest teacher to ever walk this earth: Christ. They must be taught the teachings of the Bible and live by the printed words he spoke." "I don't understand," I interrupted Godfree. "How can we teach a generation of people to change?" "Before we can make change we need to understand our history," he replied.

"Let me explain," he continued. This generation will be known as Generation Y. The first generation was known as Generation X. Our next generation will be known as Generation Z. I don't know if you understand the alphabet but there are no more letters after Z. If Generation Y doesn't prepare the changes for Generation Z, there will be no more alpha, only omega. Generation X was the generation of the '50s and '60s and part of the '70s. It was a very freethinking and open generation. They were individuals that liked to express their individuality. They challenged the system and weren't afraid to speak their mind. They were radical and crazy but they didn't know how to work together. The old saying that says there is no I in team, applies to them because they were full of eyes. They looked but didn't listen. They saw but never understood. Their vision was short-sighted and narrow. They simply couldn't work together as one. They couldn't organize themselves and work as a team. They had the ability to make great changes in the system but ultimately failed because they were more concerned with what individuals wanted to change rather than what was collectively needed to change. They lost their momentum.

"The space between original thought began to shrink. In part because of the visual language that engulfed the masses. The relationship between the visual finally caught the audio. What was being said was also being given a face, a false face. The expressions were calculated and placed by the visual teachers. Few recognized this creature and it grew rapidly in the '70s. The era of disco lights and spinning balls excited the senses and distracted many people from what corporate monsters and corrupt governments were doing. The rapid race of technology kept the mind distracted. We were captured and lost in this age of historical growth.

"Like a child moving into puberty, we marveled at our new parts and purposes. We embraced without question our video dreams. Creative language fell into a pit of technological nets, created to purposely trap and hold the minds of individuals. The '80s and '90s increased the rate of change and accelerated the amount of information downloaded. This Y generation became a people of instant gratification. They became so caught up with information that they lost the ability to think outside of the box. The ever mounting amount of information created a society of conformity and complacency. They were content to allow others to lead for them as they followed. They became great team players and worked for the good of the whole. Unfortunately, they were also impatient people that wanted everything fast. Fast food, fast games, fast work and fast fun was the flavor of the day. The senses needed to be stimulated immediately for satisfaction to be achieved.

"A beginning, middle, and an end; the X generation made the mistakes, the Y generation recognized the mistakes, and the Z generation must change the mistakes. The Y generation must bring the collective questions to the surface and prepare change for Generation Z. The X generation, the unknown, had only growth and profits in mind. They were consumed by it and never considered the repercussions of their actions. They had linear vision attached with blinders negating the truths. The Y generation must remove those blinders and open the iris to the full global picture. They must represent and collectively voice the concerns for our planet. Failure to do so is the elimination of humanity. If we fail then Generation Z will also fail."

I interrupted, "How do we do this?" "The plan is simple," he replied. "Use our senses. Taste the water, smell the air, touch the soil, listen to the animals, and open our eyes to the global damage being done each day to our earth. Damage deliberately created by man for profit and power. The earth is the connection we all share with every living being on this planet. We have the greatest responsibility placed in our opposable thumbs."

"I still don't understand how we can make people change," I asked. "Let me illustrate my point," he said. "A master teacher asked an elite group of students what were the Seven Wonders of the World. The teacher began writing their list on the chalk- board: One: Egypt's great pyramids. Two: Taj Mahal. Three: Grand Canyon. Four: Panama Canal. Five: China's Great Wall. Six: St. Peter's Basilica. But they struggled to find the seventh. So the teacher went into another classroom and asked the same question to students with perceived less intelligence. The students, dumbfounded, sat without comment until one child raised his hand. 'Lorax, you have an answer?' the teacher asked. 'Yes,' Lorax responded. 'What is your answer?' the teacher asked. 'The Seven Wonders of the World are: to touch, to taste, to see, to hear, to feel, to laugh, and the seventh wonder is to love.

"The room fell silent and the teacher was amazed.

'You are right,' the teacher replied in total bewilderment.

"We must remind people that our most precious gifts come from within ourselves. Those things that man constantly overlooks as simple and ordinary are truly wondrous," Godfree finished. "How do we convince people that our planet is more important than money?" I asked. "The challenge is to give back the basic gifts to our planet," Godfree said. "We must fight against power and greed. We must teach the next generation that a symbiotic relationship must be reached with regards to our environment and the corporate responsibility of profit. We must change human thought and behavior by the same sword they used. We must plant seeds of thought into the minds of our brothers and sisters. Give them the information that has been hidden and undisclosed. We must do what Lorax has been doing, inform people.

"God gave us the right to choose and the freedom to make our own choices. He gave us free will and we must convince our society that our free will has been taken from us. Government and corporation disguised as the truth, manipulate our thinking. So we must do the same. Take, for example, George W. Bush. He is a prime example of the corruption of government and business working together. If half of what was revealed on Michael Moore's film *Fahrenheit 9/11* was true, then what are other countries that are more corrupt doing? We must take back what was once ours and give back what was never ours to take. We allow intelligent humans to make choices but they must first be told the full truth. We allow God's gift of choice to be the instrument to slay the evil. We allow people the choice to continue to poison our planet or to stop the endless waste of life.

"Generation Y is not only the generation of questions but the generation for rebuilding. We must teach the Z generation how to make changes and begin a new language for understanding. Help them identify new syllables and consonants for communication. You now have a choice: you can walk back into the door that we entered and go home or you can leave through those sliding glass doors and finish your journey. I cannot make this choice. You must and you must do it now." I looked at the light that was beaming through the glass doors from the streetlight outside and grabbed my bag and left. I didn't say a word but only gave Godfree half a smile and a nod goodbye.

CHAPTER 8
THE CALLING

Through the glass door and onto the street my steps seemed endless and the path untold. I changed direction often and followed unknown streets. My feet became weary and my mind exhausted from the mindless traveling. I stepped into a café to have a cup of tea. "What would you like?" the waitress asked. "A clue," I responded. "A clue to what?" she asked. "A clue about where to go next," I said. She smiled and handed me a menu. "Start with this and I will return for your answer," she replied. I sat with a blank mind staring at the menu. Moments later she returned with a map and placed it on my table. If you don't have a clue maybe this map will help you find where you need to go," she said. "I need more than a map," I replied. "What can I get you?" she asked. You decide, I replied hopelessly. A smile grew across her face and she left. If she returns with Earl Grey tea, I said to myself, then she will be my guide. She returned and presented me with a large cup of tea. "What kind of tea is it?" I asked. "Ginkgo, to help you remember," she replied with a soft chuckle. "I wanted something else," I replied. "I was going to give you some Earl Grey but we are all out," she said.

"What is your name?" I asked. "Sara," she replied. "Saradipity," I blurted out. "No, Sara Onceler," she announced. "Sara, do you know where Lorax is?" I asked. "In the mountains," she replied without hesitation. "He is the reason we are out of Earl Grey tea." "You know him," I said as I straightened in my chair. "Yes, I do and why are you looking for him?" she asked. "I am on a journey to find this man," I said. "Why?" she asked. "I don't know," I replied. "If you don't know then why are you here?" she asked. "I have a key that I must give him. Will you help me find him?" I asked. "No," she replied sharply and then walked away swiftly from my table. Dazed and confused I stared at the cup of tea not knowing what to do next. I pulled out my medallion from inside my sweater and stared at it longing for it to give me an answer. "Where did you get that medallion?" Sara asked. "From a friend," I replied. She pulled out the same medallion from around her neck. "Finish your tea and I will return to help you," she said. Minutes later she returned. "Let's go," she said. "Where are we going?" I asked. "To a sermon on the mountain," she replied.

We departed from the café and began walking down the street. Not many words were spoken during our hurried travel. "Do you believe in God?" Sara asked. "I guess so," I replied. "This is not a complicated question," she replied with a sharp tongue. "Yes," I responded firmly. "Then you know that the last part of your journey is understanding how God fits in," she said. "I didn't know that," I said with a hint of sarcastic reverence. "He is the alpha and the omega and he is your spiritual guide in life. You must open your heart and allow his love to embrace you. Your journey in life will never be complete without his presence in your life. It will never be as it should unless he is in your life," she said. Suddenly we stopped and Sara looked me squarely in the eyes and said, "*Just love*. That is God's request to all of us. Just love the way he loves us. Love others the way that you wanted to be loved. Love the way God loves all the creatures on this earth," she said. Then she pointed to a church behind me on the other side of the street. "Go to the evening mass and listen to God's message," she said.

Startled and confused my feet walked alone. The sign in front of the church read "Rev John – *God's Calling*." I slowly climbed up the stairs and opened the large wooden door that took most of my strength to open. I positioned myself at the back of the church. The music began to play and it was intoxicating with vibrant sounds and tingling tones. A lady began singing softly and her voice silenced my noisy mind. When she finished a man dressed in street clothes walked onto the platform and warmly greeted everyone. He made some housekeeping announcements and then he began talking about

God. "Sometimes God shows up in our lives in really obvious ways. More often he shows up in our lives in quiet ways that we miss because of our busy lives. Our daily routines make us inattentive, distracted and unprepared for God's messages. But when you listen to God you will find four things that he will present.

"God has a D-A-R-E for us in life. D is for desire. He has a desire for you in life. He has a desire that you lead a life filled with love and happiness. God prepared a plan that was set in motion before you were born. Before he counted all the hairs on your head he had something in mind for you. God desired that you love him the way that he loves you. He also desires that you share his love with all the creatures on his earth. This is God's greatest desire for all mankind, just love. That desire can only be obtained if you are aware. A is for the awareness. You must be prepared to listen to God's message. If our lives become too busy we cannot hear his message. If we trouble ourselves with fears of the future or guilt and shame from the past we cannot hear God. Living in the moment is the only true way of listening to God. We must be aware of God's moments and he expects a response to his messages.

"R is for response. God requires that you will not only listen to his desires but that you respond by following the messages he sends us in our daily lives. It is not okay to just listen to God's message but you must reply to his desires. Our response is a critical message that we send to God. The way we behave in our daily lives and how we respond to life's simplest problems allows God to take inventory of our lives. The manner in which we conduct ourselves in the presence of others or in solitude is a great barometer to God. Our response to the relationships in our lives is also a window to indicate if God is present. When we respond to God's calling then we provide examples to others.

"E is for example. God wishes for us to follow the examples given to us by his son Jesus Christ but he also wants us to be examples to others. We must not only say the words, we must live them in every moment of every day just like his son. We can spread the good word of the Lord just by being godlike, living the life that he has asked of us. God provided and sacrificed the best example that any living being could ask for; his own child. God desires for us to respond to life like his son, our greatest example."

Rev. John spoke with passion from his heart and soul. I left the church with a glow in my body that I had never felt before. As I floated down steps, Sara grabbed my hand. "Come with me," she said. We walked across the street to a taxi. "Let's get in," she said. "There are people in this taxi," I replied. The door opened and someone from inside said, "get in." I looked inside and my eyes lit up like a Roman candle. Ismale and Rose were smiling and I embraced them with a huge hug. "I don't understand," I announced with surprise. "Don't you worry about the details," Ismale replied. "What happened?" I asked. "It's is not important," Rose replied cheerfully. I turned to Rose and gave her a kiss firmly on her lips. "Don't you leave me again,"

I said. "Wherever you go I am present," Rose said. "Where are we going now?" I asked. "To my place," Sara announced from the front seat.

The ride was filled with delightful discussions but I sensed that Ismale and Rose were not telling me something. We arrived at Sara's house and Ismale said goodbye. "Why aren't you coming in?" I asked. "We have to make preparations for tomorrow," Ismale replied. "What do you mean?" I asked harshly. "I must also go," Rose said. "Why?" I asked. "I need to see a friend," she replied. "But we just—" "But nothing," Ismale interrupted. "We will meet you in the morning," Rose said. "You promise?" I asked Rose. "Yes, I promise," she replied. I closed the taxi door and walked over to Sara. "Don't worry, you lack faith," Sara said.

An elderly lady was waiting at the door. "Welcome," she said. "This is my mother Liz," Sara announced. "How are you?" I asked. "If I were any better I would be twins," she replied. "Wow, I wished I felt that good," I replied. "You can," Liz said. "How?" I asked. "By having a cup of my tea," Liz replied. "Well bring it on and *super size* me," I said. "What is your name?" Liz asked. "My name is Q," I told her. "Q is a letter not a name," she responded. "Tell my parents that," I said. "Come in and rest," Liz said. "My mom grows her own herbs and makes teas from them," Sara said. "I can't wait to try it," I replied. Sara excused herself from the room and my eyes became heavy.

I got up from my fall and began looking back down at the battle. The man that was in the middle was now hovering over top of the raging battle. The army in the yellow seemed to be gaining ground on the silver and gold warriors. The box shape was becoming a rectangle and the blue and green warriors were losing ground. Suddenly the man hovering above let out a thundering noise like a trumpet. It began to rain and the wind howled and raged with great intensity. The men protecting the middle were firmly anchored to the ground but the silver and gold warriors were slipping and sliding uncontrollably. A second trumpet blasted in the blood-drenched night and then the rain turned to hail. The wind became a wild hurricane and it tossed the silver and gold warriors about like paper bags. The yellow soldiers turned around and faced the inside of the rectangle. They began marching toward the middle. Next the white soldiers began marching toward the middle and then the green and finally the blue soldier. They all began marching toward one another. The gold and silver warriors were all gone; not a soul left. The man hovering above gently floated back to the ground. He landed on the ground and when he did all the soldiers fell to their knees. They reached out their hand in praise. Then a pure snow-white light shot out from their outstretched fingers pouring into the man in the middle. The energy from the white light became so intense that my eyes were temporarily blinded.

Suddenly, a third trumpet pierced the crisp night air and the light disappeared. I opened my eyes to discover that all the soldiers were gone and that only the man was left standing. I felt my feet leave the ground but nothing was taking hold of me. I floated from the ledge down to the ground facing the man. His head was covered from his cloak. His arms extended toward me with his cloak covering his body. From his outstretched arm he handed me a scroll. A blast from a fourth trumpet erupted from the silent stars. I became startled and dropped the scroll to the ground. The moment the scroll reached the ground it ignited into a large flame. I instantly reached for it and my hand disappeared in the flames. I felt my skin sizzle from the heat. When my hand withdrew only a small piece of paper was saved. I quickly blew off the ashes and the words from the paper were revealed. It said "The Book of Truth and Love."

"It is ready," a faint voice cried from the distance. I opened my eyes and Liz was walking toward me with a teacup and saucer. "Did you drift off?" she asked. "Yes, I must have," I replied. "Well drink some of this and you will feel better," she said. "What is it?" I asked. "A mixture of herbs and a little organic honey," Liz said. I took a sip and my mouth began to smile with pleasure. "This is awesome," I replied. "Glad you enjoy it. How was church?" she asked. "It was very refreshing," I replied. "What was Rev. John's topic tonight?" she asked. "God's Calling," I replied. "Did God call on you?" she asked. "I am beginning to believe that he has," I responded. "Well, God has a plan for every one of his children and the key to understanding his plan is to keep an open heart. An open heart to his quiet messages and his written words," Liz proclaimed. "What do you mean?" I asked. "If you listen carefully, God will fill your heart and mind with clues to his plan for you. But unfortunately our lives become too busy and our minds too full that we never hear him," she said. "That is what Rev. John was saying. He said that God has something in mind for each of us and that we must be open to his calling," I recalled with excitement.

"Yes, God will whisper into your heart but if your life is too loud to hear him you will miss his messages," she said. "How do I know what God wants me to do?" I asked. "You need to do two things. First you need to make time in your daily life to share conversations with God and you need to learn from his written works," she said. "How do I do that?" I asked. "Each day you must have time set aside to share a quiet offering to God. You must schedule into your busy life, time with your father each day. This time is sacred time and it cannot be interrupted. It must be when you can give your full and undivided attention to him. To be fully attentive to God, you must be totally absent from you. In today's society that is difficult because we think that we are too busy and we have more important details to attend to. What can be more important than spending time with your creator each day? What is so important in our lives that can't be postponed or delayed for God?

"Second you need to understand the teaching of God's son by reading and investing in the book of truths," she replied. "What is the book of truths?" I asked. "The Bible, silly," she said. "You must learn from our greatest teacher, his son Jesus Christ. Going to the church is a wonderful first step towards building a relationship with God. But does one hour out of 168 in a week do justice to the man that created you and has the ability to give you eternal life? You really can't get to know someone if you only spend an hour a week with him or her," she said. "I guess not," I replied. "God created us and he loves us unconditionally. Which means we can sin but he wouldn't stop loving us. But he does have some standards that he expects us to live by. The Commandments and his son's teachings are a solid foundation to build from. If you keep God in your heart and open your mind to his messages, he will guide you. But you must learn how to filter out all the noise and live each moment he gave us to the fullest. You must learn how to not get lost in the past or the future," she said. I jumped up out of my chair. "That was my first doorway. I was taught to live in the moment by a young native man. It was strange because I became aware of many things when I silenced my mind," I said proudly.

"God can only speak to you when your eyes are able to see without the noise," she said. "You must be clear of the fear, shame, and guilt that the devil places in our lives. The dark one will fill our lives with these emotions so that we cannot receive God's messages. He is clever, this fallen angel, and he has convinced society that we all must work harder and live in a faster paced world. He is the one that created guilt and fear to distract us from God. But God has freed us from sin so that we wouldn't feel guilty or have any shame in our lives. God loves us and all that he desires in return is for us to love him back the same way. God invites us to engage in a relationship with him but he also gave us the free will to make that choice.

"Have you ever seen the painting with Jesus outside of a door but there is no door handle?" Liz asked. "No," I replied. "Well it represents the way God approaches his relationship with us. He can't open the door. Only we can from the inside," she said. "That is clever," I replied. "Yes, he is pretty smart that way," she said. "But why doesn't Jesus just knock on the door and let himself in?" I asked. "Your father doesn't want to impose his will on your life. His greatest joy is when his children choose of their own free will to open the door and invite him in. God wants us to be a part of his life more than anything but he will not force us to accept him. He needs to know that your heart is pure. He dares us to build a relationship with him. He dares us to love him the way he loves us. It is a journey and the passage is filled with many doors," she said. "I understand what you are saying and I have had Jesus waiting far too long. I have been opening doors. In fact, I have opened seven doorways thus far," I said. "What doorways?" Liz inquired. "Before my journey began, back in Windsor Ismale told me that I had to go through seven doors that would lead me to seven understandings in my journey. I have traveled through six and today I walked into the church for my seventh," I said.

"Seven is a powerful number. In Revelation, John speaks of the seven lamp stands and the seven stars. The seven stars are the angels and the seven lamp stands are the seven churches," she said. "What are you talking about?" I asked. "Nothing you can't read for yourself in the Bible," she replied. I began to yawn. "I am ready for a sleep," I said. "I have prepared our spare room for you," Liz replied. She brought me to my room. "Have a peaceful sleep," she said. "Thank you," I replied. I flopped on the bed and stared at the ceiling. My mind was playing ping-pong with all of my thoughts. The seven doorways, I thought to myself: the truck, the diner, the library, the train, the sweat hut, Godfree's house, and the church. Each doorway brought me to where I am now. Each lesson in life is connected and by being aware of God's intentions in my life I can begin to choose his will and not mine. Quietly, I told myself to listen for God's message. Silently, I lay down and slowly my eyelids hid into my face.

CHAPTER 9
THE CLIMB

Ismale was tugging on my feet. "Wake up you lazy toad," he said. "What are you doing here?" I asked. "It is time to prepare for your climb," he said. "What climb?" I asked. "The climb up the mountain," he replied sharply. I gathered my belongings and entered the kitchen. Liz, Sara, and Rose were all sitting at the table. "Rose," I announced cheerfully. I gave her a huge bear hug. "Good morning, my darling," I said. "Good morning, my precious," she replied. "Well, thanks for everything, Liz and Sara, but we must be on our way," Ismale proclaimed. "Thanks Liz, I will always remember our conversation that we shared," I said. She gave me a warm embrace and then she handed me a Bible. "You will need this for the rest of your journey," she said. "Yes, I will," I answered. I looked over at Rose and she smiled knowingly. We headed out the door and into a car that Ismale had rented. "Sit in the front seat with me," Ismale demanded. "Okay," I replied. "Grab a bagel and some fruit from the back seat. You are going to need your energy for the beginning of your journey," he said. "Beginning, you mean the end," I replied. He just smiled and drove away. "Where are we going?" I asked. "To find Lorax," he replied. "You know where he is?" I asked. "Yes, I do," he proclaimed. "How?" I asked. "Never mind because if I tell you I will have to shoot you and we can't have that," he said, amusing himself.

The ride was quiet and I took the time to soak in the scenery. The mountains were majestic and the beauty of God's grandeur was breathtaking. "Ismale, I have traveled through all seven doors," I said. "You have," he said sarcastically. "Yes, I have," I replied swiftly. "Well, remember your lessons and live them well. But they only represent the beginning of many doorways of awareness. You will find yourself walking through many more openings of understanding but they all begin with you turning the handle and letting the one on the other side in," he said. "You are talking about God, aren't you," I replied. "Yes, my Jedi student. Nothing is impossible with our creator. Everything you have been taught came from him. All that you are and all that you will become is his. He is the alpha and the omega. Your awareness of God in your life will allow you to gain a fuller understanding of who you are and what your purpose is on this earth."

Ismale pulled out something from his front pocket and handed it to me. "Open your hand, I have something for you that you have earned," he announced proudly. I held out my hand and he dropped a copper ring into it. I remembered when we first began this journey Ismale told me that I would receive this ring if we completed our mission. I remember calling it worthless and insignificant. I remember how rude and sarcastic I was to him. I wanted to apologize to him, I wanted to tell him I was sorry for my ignorance, but I couldn't. My eyes started to fill with water as I looked him straight in the eyes. "I am honored to accept this gift," I said choking back the tears. "You have earned this ring and it will always represent this journey and the many others that you willingly take. The significance of this ring will be explained later to you but you need to know that it is yours to keep for as long as you want."

Sirens began screaming from behind us and the police officer was gesturing for us to pull over to the side of the road. I wanted to ask Ismale what he meant about keeping the ring as long as I want. "They tracked us through the rental car," Ismale said. "What is going to happen to us?" I asked. "Nothing if you do exactly what I tell you, do you see the mountain just over there?" He pointed towards a mountain close to us. I want you to find the north face of the mountain and climb it. Lorax is staying on a landing about halfway up the mountain. He knows that you are coming and he will be looking for you. The climb is steep at times but there is a path to follow. At the base of the mountain look for a sign that says North Face Trail. Travel along that trail and Lorax will find you.

Place this yellow ribbon around your right arm." He handed me a yellow bandetta. "Now, I will distract the officer and when I do slip out of the door and hide down into that ditch. Rose, when I stop we will both jump out of the car and ask the officer for direction to the nearest hospital because you have a concussion. Q, take the bag of supplies with you and good luck my friend," he said. "Will I see you after I find Lorax?" I asked. "Most certainly, I still have to give you your name," Ismale said. "I am always with you," Rose said. "I know," I replied.

I waited until Ismale and Rose left the car and they had the police officer facing away from the car. I crawled out of the car and into the ditch and I waited about ten minutes before the police car left with Rose and Ismale in the back seat. Alone again, I thought to myself. I felt something rubbing against my back. It was the Bible that Liz had given me. I am never alone, I thought to myself. I began walking across a field toward the mountain. I arrived at the base of the mountain and decided to sit down for a moment of quiet reflection. I noticed a woman standing by herself looking up at the mountain. My gaze traveled along her view and I was amazed at the depth and breadth of the mountain. When I looked away from the mountain, I noticed that the lady was gone. I took a big breath and caught my feet.

After some searching, I found the sign for North Face Trail. I began my climb with much noise in my mind. What will I say to Lorax? What if I don't find him? Will he like me? *Stop*, I said to myself. Clear the noise and listen. I noticed the same woman from before ahead of me. She stopped and turned to me. "Where are you headed?" she asked. "I am going up North Face Trail to meet a friend," I said. "Do you like this friend?" she asked. I was stunned because I didn't know Lorax. "Why do you ask?" I replied. "Because you are on the wrong path. Your path is about twenty yards west of this path," she said. I looked at her strangely. "Are you sure?" I asked. "Yes, I live around here and I hike this mountain often," she replied. "Wow, I would have climbed all day and never gotten to my destination," I said. "Yes, you were on the wrong path," she replied. "Thank you. . ." I said, pausing for her to tell me her name. "My name is Carol," she said. "Thank you Carol, I would have never found my friend if you were not ahead of me on this path," I said. "Life is strange that way," she replied. "Imagine, I would have come all this way and on the last part of my journey and I would have been lost if it wasn't for you, Carol. Those poor souls that don't believe in divine intervention. . ." I declared as I was walking away from Carol. I found the correct path and began climbing. I thanked God quietly in my thoughts for helping me locate the right path. Then I realized that he has been helping me all along. Starting with me losing my house and finding Ismale along a path I never traveled before. The climb was inspiring and with each step I rehearsed what I was going to say to Lorax. I was trying to think of an opening line that would be profound. I was trying to think of something that would separate me from everyone else. Nothing came to mind and then I realized that I have nothing to prove because I will let God take control. I will let God do the talking. A sense of relief came over my body. I felt free and happy. Perhaps, God can make all my decisions. Perhaps, I will let him take control of my life and I will follow. Perhaps, that is God's will, I thought.

I heard something in the distance. I looked up and an eagle was in full flight. His wings were spread across the horizon and his sail was high and mighty. I watched as the eagle danced in the wind. I remember Sara holding my hand and the vision of the dove that turned into a loon that became a raven that turned into an eagle. Joy rushed into my arteries and my pace began to quicken. Without notice, I began racing up the face of the mountain with the grace of a deer in full flight. A loud shriek suddenly stopped my steps. Breathing heavily, I strained to hear over my exhausted breath. Looking up in the sky I could see the eagle proudly perched on top of the tallest mountain tree midway up the mountain. I felt the eagle's stare as he beckoned me to his position on the mountain. I began sprinting up the jagged rocks and fallen branches. I constantly looked up to gauge my position. The eagle became my compass and I his lost ship. My pace quickened the closer I approached. Suddenly, the eagle jumped from his branch and he soared over top. His wings were fully spread announcing his departure. After circling the tree he rested on, he floated into the horizon and he melted into the setting sun.

Cautiously, I began to climb again. The closer to the tree of the eagle the more silent my steps became. I noticed a ledge on the mountain and a small fire glowing. Slowly, I moved toward the fire. I stopped and positioned myself behind a bush to observe the unknown. A man arrived out of the opening in the mountain and sat next to the fire. After a few moments he yelled out, "What is your question?" Startled, I did not respond. "Are you wearing yellow?" he asked. "Yes," I replied. "So what is your question?" he asked again. "Why do people do what they do?" I asked. "Interesting question," he responded. "Come closer and sit with me for a while," he said. The warmth of the fire filled my body with a sense of relief.

"Q, is that your name?" he asked. "Yes," I replied. "Lorax?" I asked optimistically. "Yes, and are you the man with all the questions?" he replied. "Yes, I am and I am also here to save you," I said. "Save me! Save me from what?" he asked. "From all the people who are after you," I replied. He began to laugh. Was he laughing at me because I was going to be his rescuer, his savior? In between his laughter he said, "I don't need to be saved by anyone except God. Let me see the ring," he demanded. "I gave this ring to Ismale a long time ago and it was his to keep for as long as he wanted. You have been given a very special gift because that ring represents a rite of passage from one world into another." "I don't understand, why did Ismale give me the ring and what does it mean?" "Ismale gave you this ring because he believes that you are passing from the physical world to the spiritual world. He gave you this ring because he has seen your spirit and he knows of the insights you have gained and the ones you are going to make. Ismale believes in you and trusts that you will follow through on your promise." "What promise? I didn't make any promise to him." It isn't the promise you made to him specifically but to God. The promise that you will continue to seek the truth and live a life filled with his love and understanding. You will understand it more clearly later but for now you have some questions for me."

"Why are all these people searching for you? Did you do something wrong?" I asked. "Why do you assume I did something wrong?" he asked. "Because you are wanted by many government officials," I replied. "Just because they work for the government doesn't validate what they are trying to do to me. I have been exposing the corruption of our government and many large corporations. In fact, I have exposed many lies that they didn't want made public. Unfortunately, many people value power and wealth over ethics and morals. I have been able to inform many people about the injustices that have continued to plague our humanity," he said.

"What injustices?" I asked. "Our society has developed an immunity to corruption and greed. It has become socially acceptable to lie and cheat for the benefit of wealth, even though the lies and deceit directly affect the health and well-being of our own species. I will give you an example. Drug companies will sell products to consumers that they know will harm them. They will sell drugs that they know will kill some people. They will knowingly kill other humans just to increase their profits. The people we elect to serve on our behalf are protecting the same greedy individuals that are killing us. We are actually electing the bodyguards of the people that kill our neighbors, friends, and relatives.

"I need to be released from my bondage and freed from my solitude," he said. "I don't understand," I said. "You need not trouble yourself with my concerns, you have a question that you want me to answer," he replied. "Yes, I do, but . . ." He stopped me before I could go on. "Listen to me truthfully, I will tell you but we don't have much time so you cannot interrupt me, okay," he said. "Okay," I replied.

"You have learned many great lessons and you have entered doorways of knowledge on your own free will. Your willingness to learn will give you a greater understanding of people and why they do what they do. Unfortunately, it will not answer the ultimate truth," Lorax said. "What is this truth you speak of?" I asked. "It is the truths and lessons given by our creator. He has everything to do with who we are and what we do in life," he said. "I don't understand," I replied. "I must ask you a question and I need an honest response. Do you believe in God?" he asked. "Yes, I do," I responded with a slight hesitation. "Do you believe that God created the heavens and the earth and do you believe that God has a place for you in heaven?" he asked. "Of course I do but I don't know much about God and what I must do to be with him," I replied.

"Well, your lack of his words in your life can be changed. God is the light that reveals the dark. He looks for the good in all of his children. Many people believe that our time on this earth is a dress rehearsal for what roles we will receive in eternity. Like we are trying out for parts in a major Broadway production; but they are wrong. The truth is that our time on this earth isn't a dress rehearsal but the audition. No one has secured a place with God until they have accepted God in their lives. The way we live this life will determine whether or not we spend our next life with our creator or not. You want to know why people do what they do. Just ask yourself how much does the word of God exist in their lives. Man was given the ability of choice and from the beginning of time that choice has been God's greatest gift and his greatest disappointment. In the heart of every creature God has given the ability to love and that is how our time on this earth is measured.

I believe that God will ask one question before we can enter his kingdom: *How well did you love*? How well did we love God and our neighbors? It is our greatest commandment." "The greatest commandment given by God is to love?" I asked, confused. "It is recorded in the Bible, Jesus was asked what the greatest commandment of all is and he told the man to love God with all your heart, soul, mind, and strength. And equally important is to love you neighbor as yourself.

"Everything we do, we do for love. As we grow from a child to an adult we are witness to many kinds of emotions from love to hate. Each time we receive love we absorb that love into our hearts. The same holds true for hate. If we witness more love than hate, our hearts become fuller and more love can be given in return. A heart that is witness to an environment of hate, deceit, lying, adultery, drug, and alcohol abuse, cheating and stealing must protect what little love that is given. That child will behave in any manner to receive love. They will lie and cheat, deceive and deny. They will behave the same way as their parents so that they will be accepted and feel loved. Over time that heart will be filled with more and more hate and the love that they tried to protect will be put to sleep. That heart can be repaired and changed with God's love." He handed me a piece paper that was rolled up. "Read it out loud," he said.

A wicked tongue heard evil messages.
A fearful mind recorded an insecure messenger.
A tearful eye witnessed a damaged heart.
A joyful smile chose God.

"God wants us to love each other the same way he loves us," he said. "But more importantly, God yearns for us to love him. How many people do you know that love God but don't love other creatures on this earth? If a person loves God with all his or her heart then God is able to fill more love into him or her with all of his heart. A heart filled with God's love is a heart that will love others unconditionally because God loves everyone unconditionally. Our father loves us and accepts our sins by forgiving them. Even though we stumble and sometimes fall he never stops loving us. God's love is everlasting and will remove the spirit of hate. With love comes happiness. With happiness comes acceptance. Acceptance allows us to look beyond the shortcomings and misguided deeds of others. Acceptance allows us to forgive like our father. It allows us to live our lives without hate, guilt, or shame. The shackles of a wounded heart are freed because the grace of forgiveness is in it. But it all starts with God's love and his desire for us to love him and others." He finished to take a drink of water. "But how do I do all this? How do I learn to love so freely?" I asked.

"Talk to your father each day," he replied. "Learn and think of his teachings often. Quietly ask God questions throughout your day. Honor him formally by attending church and working in fellowship with others in need. Join a small group in your church and become part of his community. Finally, give your free will back to God. He has given us free will hoping that we will give it back to him. Choose to allow God to take control of your life. Have confidence that he can run your life better than you. Trust that his love will fill your life and provide a happiness that is unknown in common hour. All humans want two things in life: love and happiness. Love is all God wants in return."

Night was consuming the sky and the light of day was fading. The voices of men could be heard in the distance. Lorax noticed my panic. "Don't be afraid," he said. I looked at him and he smiled fully back at me. He placed his right arm over my shoulders. "Be at peace, you are with God. Your time has come," he said. I reached into my pocket and handed Lorax a gold key that Rose gave me. "I was told to give this to you," I said. "What is this key for?" I asked. Lorax got up slowly from his seat and began to walk back into the mouth of the mountain. "Where are you going?" I asked. "It is not my time yet, I must get lost now but you will hear from me," he said confidently. "What do I do now?" I whispered to myself. He turned to me just before he slipped out of sight and said,

"It is time for you to get *lost too.*"

The End

The second book of this trilogy is called "**Lost with Lorax**." The third book will be entitled "**Leaving in Lorax**." The material for the second book is almost completed.

Working Towards Eternity
Rick Dugal

Printed in the United States
104365LV00001B/103/P